LOVE AMONG
THE RUINS

LOVE AMONG THE RUINS

A MEMOIR OF LIFE AND LOVE IN HAMBURG, 1945

HARRY LESLIE SMITH

ICON

Published in the UK in 2015
by Icon Books Ltd,
Omnibus Business Centre,
39–41 North Road,
London N7 9DP
email: info@iconbooks.com
www.iconbooks.com

Originally published in 2012 under
the title *Hamburg 1947: A Place
for the Heart to Kip* by Barley Hole
Press, Belleville, Ontario

Sold in the UK, Europe and Asia
by Faber & Faber Ltd,
Bloomsbury House,
74–77 Great Russell Street,
London WC1B 3DA or their agents

Distributed in the UK, Europe
and Asia by TBS Ltd,
TBS Distribution Centre,
Colchester Road, Frating Green,
Colchester CO7 7DW

Distributed in South Africa
by Jonathan Ball,
Office B4, The District,
41 Sir Lowry Road,
Woodstock 7925

Distributed in Australia and
New Zealand
by Allen & Unwin Pty Ltd,
PO Box 8500,
83 Alexander Street,
Crows Nest, NSW 2065

Distributed in India
by Penguin Books India,
7th Floor, Infinity Tower – C,
DLF Cyber City,
Gurgaon 122002,
Haryana

Distributed in Canada
by Publishers Group Canada,
76 Stafford Street,
Unit 300,
Toronto,
Ontario M6J 2S1

Distributed to the trade
in the USA
by Consortium Book Sales
and Distribution
The Keg House,
34 Thirteenth Avenue NE,
Suite 101,
Minneapolis,
MN 55413-1007

ISBN: 978-178578-000-4

Typeset in Monotype Bell by Marie Doherty

Printed and bound in the UK by Clays Ltd, St Ives plc

Contents

For Friede: 1928–1999

Who was my love, my faith, my Heimat …

About the author

Harry Leslie Smith's *Guardian* articles have been shared almost a quarter of a million times on Facebook and have attracted huge comment and debate. His book *Harry's Last Stand* (Icon, 2014) received widespread praise, with Annie Lennox saying that Harry 'is absolutely one of my heroes. Everyone should read this and be humbled.' He lives in Yorkshire.

Acknowledgements

I would like to extend my thanks to the Bundesarchiv in Berlin, Germany, and the Hamburg City archives for allowing me to utilise their resources. Their assistance was invaluable in writing this book. I cannot express enough gratitude to my friends and my wife's closest confidantes, Gerda Metzler and Ursula Overbeck, for their insights and assistance in my research about life in Hamburg during the 1930s. Your loyalty and your love, throughout the years to your friend Friede, is an inspiration. I am truly grateful to the kindness you have both shown me over the years.

I should also like to express my gratitude to the readers of my memoir *1923*, who encouraged me to continue my journey into my past. I extend my thanks to my children and my grandchildren for having supported me in my endeavours to unravel our shared history. Vickie, Melanie and Cynthia, your thoughtful reading of my manuscript and your corrections have added immeasurably to the quality of my memoir. I am touched by the kindness and friendship you have all shown me.

I would also like to thank some men from long ago: Sid, Dave, Taffy, and Jack for being my mates. I hope you all found your way and grabbed some happiness out of this all too short a life.

I must also acknowledge my appreciation and thanks to: Walker, Locke and Cox; who were not only decent officers, but thoroughly decent men. They always did their best and deserve to be remembered for their empathy towards their fellow man.

Finally, I acknowledge my gratitude to all those people I have broken bread with while on this Earth. I hope your life was enriched as much as mine was by your company.

To the reader

It is autumn and it is wet and damp outside. I can already feel the approaching cold and heavy breath of the frozen months upon the nape of my neck. If I survive, this will be my 92nd winter on this Earth. Some say age brings wisdom, reason, serenity. I say bollocks; great age brings rheumatism, deafness, vascular degeneration and organ failure. So far, I have been lucky and my body has endured my storm-tossed life healthy and intact. It is a blessing I appreciate and honour every morning by performing the graceful movements of tai chi, which provides me the balance to combat the punishment that great age bestows on those who dare to live so long. We suffer the irretrievable loss of love, through death. We abide the profound loneliness of age as friends and lovers disappear from our grasp and are replaced with static photographs mounted high up on our fireplace mantel. I don't ask for condolences or your pity because I have felt an elemental chart of wondrous emotions during my life. I have experienced the very best and the very worst that mankind has to offer. I have loved and been loved and that is a great matter. It is all that should matter. It is all that must matter, even to you, dear reader. So as I walk into the fourth season of life, I say accept love as it comes and accept love as it goes because it is the only currency that never devalues us.

I leave you now with a small piece of my life; my time in Germany following the last Great War. It is a simple story about people searching to belong and survive in a world that was almost destroyed.

Cheers,
Harry Leslie Smith

CHAPTER 1

1945: The conditions of surrender

I don't know why, but the winter rains stopped and spring came early in 1945. When Hitler committed suicide at the end of April, the flowers and trees were in full bloom and the summer birds returned to their nesting grounds. Not long after the great dictator's corpse was incinerated in a bomb crater by his few remaining acolytes, the war in Europe ended. After so much death, ruin and misery, it was remarkable to me how nature resiliently budded back to life in barns and fields and across battlegrounds, now calm and silent. The Earth said to her children: it is time to abandon your swords and harness your ploughs; the ground is ripe and this is the season to tend to the living.

I was 22 and ready for peace. I had spent four years in the RAF as a wireless operator. I was lucky during the war; I never came close to death. While the world bled from London to Leningrad, I walked away without a scratch. Make no mistake, I did my part in this war; I played my role and I never shirked the paymaster's orders. For four years, I trained, I marched, and I saluted across the British Isles. During the final months of the conflict, I ended up in Belgium and Holland with a unit that was responsible for maintaining abandoned Nazi airfields for Allied aircraft.

When Germany surrendered to the Allies in gutted Berlin, I was in Fuhlsbüttel, a northern suburb of Hamburg.

At the time, I didn't think much about Fuhlsbüttel, I felt it was between nothing and nowhere. It was much like every other town our unit drove through during the dying days of the war. Nothing was out of place and it was quiet, clean, and as silent as a Sunday afternoon. Our squadron took up a comfortable residence in its undamaged aerodrome.

While I slept in my new bed in this drowsy neighbour-hood, the twentieth century's greatest and bloodiest conflict came to an end at midnight on 7th May. On the morning of the 8th, our RAF commander hastily arranged a victory party for that afternoon. The festivities were held in a school gymnasium close to the airport.

The get-together might have been haphazard and the arrangements made on short notice, but there were no complaints because death was now a postponed appointment. Our individual ends, from road accidents, cancer, or old age, were to be pencilled in for a date in the far distant future. There was a lot of excitement, optimism and simple joy generated during the party because we were young and pissed on free beer. RAF officers, NCOs and enlisted men marked the passage from war to peace, dancing the bunny hop in the overheated school gymnasium.

No one considered or asked on that day of victory, 'What happens next?' That was tomorrow's problem. I certainly didn't question my destiny on that spring afternoon. Instead, like the Romans, I followed the edict: *carpe diem.* I ate too much, I smoked too much, and I drank too much. And why not?, I reasoned. The war was over and I had survived, whereas a great many had been extinguished as quickly as blowing out a flame on a candle.

I still didn't want to think about tomorrow, even when our victory party was no more than a hungover echo of patriotic songs and dirty limericks playing inside my head; I was content to wait and watch. I was perfectly happy to observe my mates plod onwards like dray horses back to their old lives. I was satisfied to enjoy a moment that wouldn't last, peace without obligation. I relished the mundane luxury of sitting on a bench with a cigarette between my fingers. I indulged in the sensual pleasure of feeling the warm spring sun hover over my face. I was liberated from home and the dismal dull world of a mill town, where one's life was charted to end as it began: in a tenement house, under grey, dense skies. I wanted to simply enjoy and savour my release from the threat of death.

During those first few days of peace, I was overwhelmed with a feeling of good fortune. It was really blind luck that I had endured. My survival was the mythical lucky dip at a fairground raffle. I was alive while millions of combatants and civilians simply perished in this long and brutal conflict.

It wasn't long after road workers had swept the streets clean from our victory parade that I began to realise my four years of service to the state hadn't altered me greatly. Perhaps I was a bit more educated and less naive about the world. I had certainly acquired some now-redundant skills in marching and Morse code. I was also more aware that suffering and hurt was not a commodity in short supply. Possibly an outsider might have even considered me more cynical and crass after my years with the RAF. Yet underneath my cocksure attitude I was still the same self-conscious, lonely, awkward teenager who had volunteered to join the RAF in December 1940.

No matter how relieved I felt with Hitler dead and peace at hand, it reminded me that my personal destiny was now my own responsibility. Considering that the war had rescued me from the nightmare of my past life, I was a bit frightened by peace. I was comfortable in my RAF blue uniform, which made me look the same as Bill Jones, Will Sanders, or a multitude of other boys from counties all across Britain. I didn't want to be Harry Smith from Halifax, former manager at Grosvenor's Grocers, son of a cuckold, from the backside of town.

So for as many moments as I could grasp, I took smug comfort in the anonymity of military life. I relished the new laid-back approach both officers and NCOs took to commanding our group. It was a simple decree to live and let live. As long as there was no scandal, we were allowed to pursue our own pastimes for amusement or profit.

As the spring dissolved into summer, I began to appreciate that the war had been relatively harmless and uneventful for me. My life must change, I ventured, because I was one of the fortunate few; I was healthy and alive. The question was how to modify the existence that had been laid out for me since my parents' rapid and one-way journey into poverty and rough living.

While shaving one morning in the wash hut, I said to my mate Dave: 'I don't know what to do with myself. I don't want to be working at a mill back in Halifax or be a grocer.'

Dave took a while to reply because he was absorbed in taking careful strokes around his chin with a razor. 'It's all in the cards you are dealt before you are born. Some get a lucky hand while others get shite. If all you get dealt is deuces, there's nothing you can do about it, except learn how to fucking bluff.' Dave paused, looked at his clean face, and added as an afterthought to the rules for a successful life: 'You also need a good fry up in the morning.'

Was he right? Was it just down to luck? He might have been on to something. So far, every direction my life had taken was a simple act of chance or whimsy. After all, flat feet and a flaccid patriotic sentiment led me to the doors of the RAF. Most likely, had I picked another branch of the armed forces, I would have ended up as a name stencilled on a cenotaph to be washed in the indifferent rain falling on Halifax. So, for the present, I left my life in the hands of fortune reinforced by bullshit.

On the days I was permitted to leave our base, I strolled until my legs ached, exploring my surroundings as if they were the ruins of Troy. To remain alive in 1945, the Germans were reduced to the most primitive form of commerce: they bartered and begged, and they did it in every imaginable location. I encountered Germans in back alleys, on street corners, or by the entrance to the train station, huddled in small groups trading their heirlooms for food.

In the beginning, I was emotionally detached from Germans and the destruction around me. Their suffering played as blandly as a sepia-toned newsreel at the Odeon cinema. The immensity of the pain endured by both the innocent and the damned was too much for me to absorb. What lay outside of my privileged life in camp was a festering sore that fouled the air. I tried to keep my distance from the Germans and their troubles.

Keeping my heart cold and lofty didn't last long because I was a young man looking for a bit of emotional adventure. Within two weeks, I was trying to start conversations with young German women. When I called out, 'Excuse me, Fräulein,' most walked by me or jumped over to the other side of the street. Some women smiled politely or giggled to their girlfriends at my bad accent and limited vocabulary.

This game ended for me on the day I travelled up Langenhorner Chaussee, in Fuhlsbüttel. It was a road populated with attractive two- and three-storey apartments, which were shaded by linden and cherry trees. It was a middle-class neighbourhood that stretched towards the horizon in relaxed prosperity. The street was a quiet and pleasant quarter that seemed immune from the tragedies unfolding all around it. It wasn't until I walked further up the road that I discovered no district in Germany was inoculated against hunger.

On the other side of the street, a commotion was brewing between an elderly man and a young woman. They were haggling over the value of a silver fork for a packet of cigarettes. I loitered and observed them struggling to barter their way out of starvation and ruin. Suddenly, I noticed a woman who made my heart and head stumble in aroused confusion. It appeared she was also bartering for food, but there was something different in her body language. It suggested to me a dignity and a pride that wouldn't yield to her circumstances.

Extraordinary, I thought; and I said aloud, 'You are

beautiful.' Afterwards, I did something rash: I displayed a confidence I generally lacked, unless full of beer. I barged into the young woman's life. It was reckless, it was foolish, and perhaps it was even desperate. It also proved the extent of my loneliness and my habitual foolishness to fall in love with foreign things. During our first encounter, she was moderately indifferent to my entreaties. Perhaps she was even amused by my stilted German and my pushy courteousness. On instinct, or possibly it was a girlish whim because I seemed harmless, she graciously allowed me to walk her part-way home.

'What's your name?' I asked.

'Elfriede Gisela Edelmann,' she quickly responded.

I tried to repeat the name, but it jumbled out horribly wrong.

She laughed and said, even though we weren't yet friends, 'Call me Friede, it is easier.'

I must have left a favourable impression because Friede agreed to meet me for a picnic the following week. So began my slow and irresolute courtship with this extraordinary German woman.

Perhaps the term 'woman' was too advanced because she was only a teenager. However, at seventeen, Friede had more style, sophistication and charm than anyone I'd ever met, dated, or simply lusted after. She possessed a sense of mystery because there was something unknowable and impenetrable about her personality. It was as if there was a sunspot against her soul. Perhaps Friede created this emotional no-man's-land around herself because she had encountered evil in Hitler's Germany, or perhaps because she harboured some unhappy family secret. Whatever the reason, she was an enigma who was hard to fathom, but easy to love.

It was primal, it was emotional, and it was natural, but I wanted to get to know her better. I also wanted to sleep with her and I would do anything to get to that end. At first I took her on innocent picnics. I snatched food and wine from the RAF mess hut for our meals. I believed I was being cavalier. I thought Friede might even consider me cosmopolitan when I lit our cigarettes like Paul Henreid for Bette Davis, in the movie *Now, Voyager.* She only smiled or laughed lightheartedly at my decorum. Initially, I didn't understand that she lived in a completely different world than mine. Her universe had more immediate problems and concerns than if the wine was chilled. After a while, I began to understand that her community was in serious trouble and was suffering from a severe lack of food and medicine.

It was during an afternoon lunch on the banks of the Alster River that some of her real misfortunes and sorrow crept up on me. While she sunned her bare legs, I noticed they were covered in tiny blisters and ulcers. Friede registered my awkward stare and smiled.

'We have no vitamins, liebchen. There's nothing left to eat: all of Germany will die from scurvy, like we are on a polar expedition.'

'Why don't you have any vitamins?' I innocently asked.

Friede explained that for most Germans, the last year of the war had been very difficult. Their cities suffered round-the-clock bombardment, while the Allied armies began a massive land offensive against their nation. In the final

8

months of the war, food supplies for ordinary citizens ran out. Friede and her family lived off a soup that tasted like rainwater and ate bread made from animal feed.

'After the Russians crossed the Oder River in January 1945,' Friede explained, 'everyone knew the war was lost. It was only a matter of time before we got a taste of our own medicine. I was terrified because I didn't know who our new masters would be: Russia or America?'

'It was a good thing we Brits got here first before the Russians could get their hands on Hamburg,' I replied.

Friede laughed at my simplistic response and retorted, 'It is sometimes hard to tell if Britain is the best jailer. You British treat everyone as if they are Nazis and deserve to be punished.'

'How do we do this?' I asked.

Friede looked at me and smirked. 'Our rations are table scraps for a dog. People are expected to remove rubble from the cities, but are allotted just 1,200 calories of nutrition per day. Britain keeps my people on the edge of starvation. Have you seen the bread they give us?' she demanded angrily.

I had seen Germans queue impatiently for this almost-inedible food. At one time, I had even witnessed soldiers toss dense bricks of blackened dough to hungry crowds. It was a miserable ration to feed anyone. The ingredients were a dubious mixture of sawdust and salt, with a trace amount of flour that bonded the indigestible product together. The bread was baked in the morning and if you didn't consume it by late afternoon, a thick green mould would burrow its way to the crust. Sometimes, I caught sight of vagrants in the shadow of bomb-damaged buildings who had somehow got their hands on the thick, rotten bread. Famished, they would stuff it into their mouths and wash it back with water scooped from the street gutters.

Friede said that many believed the victors treated Germany like they did in 1918. 'The Allies will let the German people starve to death.'

'What do you mean?' I asked defensively.

'Unless you are wealthy, you can't buy food anywhere in the city. Mutti must travel north up into the countryside,' Friede told me in a halting voice. 'She sells our belongings to the farmers who give her a few eggs and a rotting turnip in exchange. How will we live once all of her jewels and silver are gone? Mutti says the farmers act like pirates. They have no pity on the city folk and will rob you of everything you own for a morsel of food. People say the farmers are rich from the city's misery and have Persian carpets in their pigsties.'

Afterwards, I thought my invitation to a lunch by the river seemed nothing more than a cynical gesture. I blamed myself for not understanding her difficulties sooner because I had endured a similar hunger in my childhood.

My growing affection for Friede drove me to become a conspirator in her survival. I obtained food for Friede and her family by the old and reliable methods my mother had taught me: if you can't buy it, beg for it, and if you can't beg for it, nick it while God and the holy ghosts are down at the pub. So, from storage units on our base, I snatched anything I thought useful to them, from food rations to soap and medicine. I wrapped up the contraband in a blanket and smuggled it out of camp in a haversack.

Perhaps I was correcting the wrong done to me as a starving boy? Perhaps I was buying love and loyalty with a loaf of bread? I didn't know or care. I knew winter was coming and without someone like me, her family would starve to death like thousands of other Germans, hobbled by this devastating war.

Looking back, I think the start of our romance – the picnics by the river, the afternoons spent loitering in riverfront cafés – were just a pleasant diversion for Friede and her friends. They were an excuse to eat delicacies and savour flavours long absent from an ordinary German's diet. In the beginning, Friede didn't appreciate the ardour of my passion, but enjoyed my diligence and loyalty in trying to please her ordinary desires and satisfy her most basic needs. I was able to provide Friede with food and protection in a nation that had been cast out of civilisation. It was my sheer persistence to keep her sated and healthy with purloined wine, preserves and medicine that allowed me to ingratiate myself to her. I was able to transform our relationship from the formal *Sie* to the more hopeful and friendly *du*.

It was easy for me to fall in love with Friede because she was as glamorous as a movie star. She had deep, expressive hazel eyes, and raven hair that hung voluptuously to her shoulders. Her face was sensuous and, at times, mysterious as it expressed deep emotions and indefinable longing.

With my background of poverty, infidelity and family betrayal, Friede was everything I couldn't aspire to in England. Her education, her taste, her style were vastly more sophisticated then my Woolworths' tuppence upbringing. Being arm-in-arm with her, I felt like I was a lead character in a Saturday morning movie serial. I fell hard for Friede and plunged into the deep end of German life under occupation. Yet the bottomless, almost un-navigable water of love in a ruined nation was my best option for a better future. It was certainly better than returning to a wet and dreary existence in Britain.

Unfortunately, Friede wasn't as easily convinced of my long-term suitability as either suitor or provider. In the beginning, my loyalty and my love were chided as unproven and a childish fancy. Besides, she said, 'Tommies come and go; you too will leave for England and go back to your English girlfriend.'

I protested, but she was right – the end of my time in the RAF was nigh. Demobilisation of soldiers and airmen was moving at a steady pace. If I didn't act quickly, I was going to find myself demobbed and marching in a victory parade leading me right to the dole queue. If I truly loved Friede, as I so often claimed after a half-bottle of Riesling, I would have to find a means to remain in Germany. My only option was to extend my services with the RAF.

CHAPTER 2

Staying on

Considering that I came from the rough streets of Barnsley, Bradford and Halifax, extending my term with the RAF was an easy decision. There was nothing in Yorkshire for me except the dead footfall of orphaned hopes and dreams. I had neither an education nor a vocation. Before the war, I had been a manager at Grosvenor's Grocers in Halifax. Prior to my departure for military service, the owner had promised me that my position would be available at war's end. A lot can happen in four years and promises made in patriotic fervour are kept as seldom as New Year's resolutions. My old job was no longer available. It had been taken by a conscientious objector who dodged the draft but never an excuse to make a pound.

By the age of 22, I had an empirical certitude that there was nothing for me in England. Everything I cared for had been destroyed by the Great Depression. My father had spent his last years alone in a doss house and died a pauper. As for my mother, Lillian, she was still alive, but our relationship had been tested and damaged by extreme poverty. She secretly defied the conventions of our working-class heritage by having a love affair with a former cowman named Bill Moxon, while still married to my father.

Sometime between my seventh and eighth birthday, the cowman replaced my Dad in both my mother's heart and her bed. However, there was no happy ending for them, for my Dad or my sister and me. You see, outside our ramshackle house, the Great Depression descended like a plague upon Yorkshire. My world, along with that of the rest of Britain's poor, became a dog-eat-dog existence. I spent my youth flitting from one slum to the next, grabbing my education on the run and feeling that my future was to end in a miserable squat. I knew that the war had saved me, and in peace I was not going to return quietly to a life of rank poverty or into my mother's emotionally unstable gravitational pull.

So, it never crossed my mind to move back to my mother's because it would have been as distasteful to me as returning to a crime scene. The only emotion I had for my mother was despair. As for Halifax – the city my family came to call home after we had lived a vagabond existence that took us from Barnsley to Bradford and many points in between – it only elicited in me an overwhelming feeling of stale disappointment. Therefore to return, after my stint in the RAF, to the tenement my mother shared with her cowman and my two younger half-brothers would have been a step backwards into the grey world of the 1930s.

In 1945, I had no attachments to Britain except for one person who still tugged at my shirt-sleeves: my sister Mary. She was my true friend and companion through our family's bleakest and saddest moments. But my affection for her wasn't strong enough for me to flee back into the oppressive and stifling arms of Britain's West Riding.

Besides, Mary didn't have the means to put me up, even if I did want to return home. She lived on the steep hills of Low Moor, in a tiny terraced house with a young son and a troublesome husband. Nor did Mary have any influence with the local powers to find me employment; without a friendly word in a manager's ear there was no possibility of a job. The mills around Bradford and Halifax were brimming with unemployed servicemen, all looking to return to their old positions. If I went home, I would be just another redundant cog in the broken wheel of British industry.

Just to make sure I wasn't under any delusion about life back in Yorkshire, Mary wrote to me: 'Luv, there's nothing here for ya. There's nothing at all, no housing and certainly no brass. If you need it, I can always lend you a spare shilling. But I suspect you've got more than me, being in the RAF. But I won't deny you anything I've got; which is love and a shoulder to cry on. Stay put, stay safe and stay out of our Mam's way or she'll be asking for something from you. Enjoy your time abroad because you've got nowt to come home to.'

So there was nothing and no one to return to in post-war Britain. I knew I was more welcome walking outside the gates of our encampment down Zeppelin Strasse than on Broad Street in Halifax. So I was content to be across the North Sea in a foreign and defeated country. In fact, I was better off stationed in this desperate and ruined nation than in Britain. At least in Germany I was a member of the conquering legion. The RAF protected me from want and hunger. In exchange, I accepted that my life was theirs to waste in battle or in peace. However, in the spring of 1945, it was unlikely that the RAF was going to collect on the balance owed them. My life wasn't in any immediate danger in Europe and I wasn't going to remind them about the battles still under way in Asia.

Some of my mates had different notions about self-preservation and suggested I join them on an insane venture in the war against Japan. Their mission involved a self-propelled, one-man submarine in the South China Sea; the sub would affix limpet mines to the remnants of the Land of the Rising Sun's merchant marine. The scheme and their rationale – 'Be a bit more of a laugh than hanging around 'ere' – was lunatic at best and suicidal at worst. Considering that since my induction in the RAF, I had avoided volunteering for anything that might shorten my life with as much rigour as I ducked Sunday church parade, I wasn't going to break my lucky streak by accepting a suicide mission to the Far East, just to satisfy our dying empire or my more patriotic, testosterone-driven mates.

No, I wasn't going anywhere dangerous. I would remain in Germany because they were defeated, broken and submissive. It was the safest place in the world for me to figure out what I wanted to do with my life. I knew I wasn't cut out to live as my parents did on bread, drippings and bitter. Besides, staying on allowed me the time to pursue Friede. I wanted the opportunity to win Friede to my heart and I believed it was going to be like most of the crooners' love songs that played on Armed Forces Radio at the time – a beautiful melody that ended happily ever after.

Now that hostilities were over, the RAF had minimal expectations for the lower ranks. Their one simple rule was: keep your head down and your nose out of other people's business. I had no problem with this unwritten regulation as I had followed this practice since boyhood. As long as it didn't affect my immediate well-being, the petty affairs of others didn't rouse any interest in me. It was safer to close my eyes to everyone's evil or saintly exploits.

After all, if I wished to remain in Germany, there was wisdom in silence. I wanted to be known and relied upon for my indifference to the comings and goings of the world around me. Keeping out of trouble was one thing, trying not to witness trouble was impossible. Two weeks into our stay in Fuhlsbüttel and the profiteers were salivating at the opportunity to plunder an occupied country with no inventory list. Supplies from food to fuel were always going missing. One morning, a sergeant put a friendly arm around my shoulder after I noticed a group of airmen suspiciously hanging around a store house. The NCO said: 'Lad, keep your eyes shut and whistle a friendly tune because there's nowt to see here.'

The men I encountered were shifting boxes of tinned meats, preserves and beer into an Air Force van, which when loaded took off for an unknown destination. Later on, I mentioned the truck with its cargo of RAF stores to a hut mate and friend named Sid.

'Oh that,' he said. 'It's a sergeant's fiddle. He's got some deal with a bloody Nazi who owns a restaurant. The sergeant provides him booze and meat. In return, good old Fritz pays him in gold coins and jewellery.'

'What happens to the baubles?' I asked foolishly.

'The missus flogs it back in Leeds.'

My mouth opened up to respond, when Sid said to me: 'Don't even think of joining that party, mate. It's best we stick to what we know: getting pissed and getting laid. Everything else is a big boy's game.'

'Too right,' I agreed.

So in the interest of self-preservation, I did what I was told. I turned a blind eye to my equals and my betters. I turned my back to anything that appeared out of sorts. I even closed my ears to the sound of coins being counted in the darkness by those who were plundering the German nation or the British armed forces. However, as the weeks progressed, it became more difficult to ignore the racket caused by the pilfering. It seemed anything of value, if it wasn't guarded or nailed down, was nicked. Some members of my squad acted as if they had found bits of a Spanish galleon washed up on shore when they returned from a trip into Hamburg.

'Jesus wept, would you get a look at that watch. It only cost me a carton of bloody Lucky Strikes.'

'Jim, if you'd spent forty years in the pit as a ripper, you'd still not get a watch as fine as you traded today, for a bunch of bloody fags.'

With a nation being hawked away for cigarettes, I wasn't going to be left out of this burglary. I took what wasn't mine, but I reasoned it was an altogether different type of crime. My larceny was innocent of profit or malice. I simply pinched food for the German girl and her family. My misdemeanour was insignificant except to those that received my food parcels. I thought my actions were more akin to extending the hand of British philanthropy towards the less fortunate.

On base, there were a few others like me, unwilling to profit from the misery of others. We were incapable of seeing a reason to garner personal gain from the sunken and ashen faces of bomb-battered ordinary Germans. As for the rest, the temptation for theft and for sex without responsibility was overwhelming. It was too easy for them to suspend their morality while abroad. They believed that their ethics could resume upon their return to Britain. They thought their moral code was like a light switch; it could be turned on or off without ever marking their soul.

Within my barracks, a great many used food and cigarettes as a bartering device for nameless sex with near-starved German teenagers. Others traded food for gold, jewellery and other valuable commodities, which they saved for their return home to Brighton or Birmingham as chocolate soldiers on parade. Their dubious earnings from fraternising with the desperate provided a valuable addition to a down-payment on a house or a new car. Others just frittered their money and morality away as if they were down at their local pub with their pay packet.

'For a bit of coffee or nylons, you can get those Fräuleins to do anything you want.'

'Smith, why don't you try it, if only for a laugh? You'll never get a chance like this again, ever in your sorry life.'

But I shook my head. I had already experienced life at the hands of ghetto kings back in Bradford and had no wish to become a proper bastard in Germany. 'Sorry, lads, I don't want anything from the bloody Germans because they're nothing but trouble,' I remarked.

Someone at the far end of our hut shouted out: 'We got Jesus of the Nazarenes sleeping beside us. Let's hope he doesn't go to turning tables at temple on Sunday.'

I laughed. 'Bugger you, mate. There will be no water

into wine for you ungrateful lot.' I went back to reading my book.

A few days later, I spoke with my friend Taffy. 'I wonder if things had worked out different in the war and Jerry was on our High Street buying us out for a thruppenny, how we'd take it?'

Taffy was Welsh and as sentimental as me. I liked him for his love of poetry and whisky, and his soft touch for hard-luck stories.

'Pack it in, Harry,' Taffy said. 'Most of those lads are like us; since the day they were born they've been beaten down by the squire, by the church, and by the foreman. All they want is to taste a bit of the good life after being cheated out of it for centuries by those Tory bastards back home. Sure, they shouldn't be filching, whoring, and acting like clowns on parade just because no one gives a toss. But I'll keep schtum to their misdemeanours and leave it up to God to decide who's guilty and who's innocent.

'As for Ali Baba over there and his forty thick thieves; leave 'em be. Germany is a land of louts and I'll be glad when I am rid of it and back home in Wales. You should go home too. Forget this place; it's filled with bloody foreigners.'

Even though it disgusted me, Taffy was right about the pilfering. So I kept quiet. I didn't want my larceny to be revealed or curtailed, or for me to be punished for helping the German girl.

It was both terrifying and exciting keeping Friede's family afloat while the former German nation collapsed around us like a block of condemned buildings. It was also a giant fraud because my gallantry was circumstantial. I only appeared successful and confident to Friede because her country was decimated. Every day, I was frightened that Friede would discover my counterfeit, that my ability to save her was limited to my present circumstances. Anywhere else, I would have been just one of a hundred men, searching for work and shelter.

It scared me to think that Friede or anyone else might discover that my outward confidence was a swindle, a deception as devious as a cheque written on a bank account with a nil balance. So, there was no turmoil in my soul when I made an appointment with my superiors to extend my days in Germany. I had only one anxiety: that perhaps the RAF didn't want me and were prepared to chuck me over the side, once my terms of service were complete.

Before my scheduled appointment, I made sure that I was properly groomed. A German barber cut my hair and shaved me with a straight-edge razor. My uniform was pressed by a woman who worked at the base laundry. I was determined that my outward appearance would convince any officer that I was born for the military life. After a quick cigarette behind a Nissen hut, I marched over to the group captain's office where I was to meet with his adjutant. When I arrived, the foyer was littered with other men in similarly pressed uniforms. We looked like lackeys begging for favours in the Sun King's antechamber. The adjutant had a wiry LAC (leading aircraftman) for a secretary, who acted more like a guard dog on an estate than an administrative clerk.

I announced myself to the secretary, who scanned a large appointment book for my details. Out loud, he called out a roll of names pencilled in for meetings with the adjutant: 'Benson, Hearn, Simpson, ah yes, and here we are, Smith. Your appointment is at 1:45. Bit eager, aren't we?' he said.

'Pardon?'

'You're early for your appointment.'

'It's only five minutes away,' I pointed out.

The clerk looked up at the wall clock, back to his wrist-watch, and then smiled at me. 'You're still early. Please take a seat.'

The secretary returned to his duties and I was left to watch the minute hands from the clock make five slow revolutions. At 1:45, the clerk robotically stood from his desk and knocked on the officer's door. He entered and returned to the foyer.

'The adjutant is ready to see you.'

I stood up and the secretary admonished me.

'Come on now, let's get a move on, chop, chop. We don't have all day; the adjutant is a busy man. It's not like going to see the parson, you know.'

The secretary announced me to Flight Lieutenant Locke, the adjutant. 'Wireless Operator Smith to see you, sir.'

The officer was at his desk signing papers; behind him was a wall map of northern Germany. He looked up from his work and said, 'At ease, Smith.'

He had a waxed moustache and was at least ten years older than me. It was a kind but weary face. I noticed he was wearing a wedding band. On his desk were framed photographs of a blonde-haired woman and a little girl.

He pulled open my file, read it quickly and said: 'So you

want to stay on in Germany. Any reason for this? I hope this isn't about a girl.'

'No, sir,' I said. 'I like the Air Force and I enjoy the life. I think I can contribute to my country better in uniform than out.'

He looked back at my service record. 'You've never been up on charges and you've always passed your courses in the top percentiles. I've never heard anyone say a bad word about you. So you must be the decent sort. Well, I'm not going to deny this request. We are demobbing so many men these days, there is hardly anyone left trained to boil a kettle for tea. I'll have your request approved.'

I saluted the officer. He returned it with a sloppy hand-to-head motion. I left the office, relieved; I had bought myself six more months of time with Friede.

When Taffy saw me, he asked, 'So are you in or are you out?'

'Back in,' I responded.

'Bloody fool,' he said. 'Everyone is begging to get out of this nut house and you are climbing to get back in. Well, Smith, since you know you've got a pay packet for the next six months, let's go out on the town and get pissed.'

CHAPTER 3

A summer in the ruins of Troy

During that spring and summer of 1945, history's forge was busy. Russia and America were intent on beating out a new and different Europe from the dead Nazi era. The Potsdam Conference formally divided Germany into four unequal parts. Naturally, Russia and America, being the strongest and wealthiest partners in the war against Germany, occupied most of the country's land mass. The smaller contributors to the war effort were offered a reduced share of the fatherland. Britain was given a small but meaty portion of northern Germany. France was tossed some offal to assuage their Gallic pride. In this divided Germany, peace was strained between the Western powers and Russia, except when it came to reparations. On that subject, each occupying nation acted like an appellant at an insolvency court hearing.

Russia was by far the most brutal and vengeful occupier, having suffered greatly at the hands of Hitler's armies. So, without regret, the Soviets gnawed and chewed into their share of the German carcass that stretched from Berlin on a north–south axis and eastwards to the rich farmlands of Pomerania. Trains left on the hour destined for Moscow, filled with dismantled factories and laboratories, and heavy machinery. Along with the spoils of war, these trains also carried former Wehrmacht soldiers and the SS, condemned to Siberian hard labour.

The situation didn't look much better for Germans residing in the Western-occupied zone of their country. The Allies implemented the Morgenthau plan, which was created to neuter Germany's warlike tendencies and transform it into a pastoral society. The country's industrial base, its steel works, automobile plants and consumer manufacturing centres were dismantled. The contents of Germany's economic greatness were shipped to the Allied victors in giant rail cars and ocean freighters. Like the communists, Britain, America and France called the looting of Germany 'reparations for the just'.

As acetylene torches dismembered factories, steel mills and shipyards across Germany, so the friendships I had built in the RAF were also being dismantled. One by one, my mates departed and their names were replaced on the sergeant's morning roll call roster with new and unfamiliar draftees. My friends went home to their old and familiar civilian lives, while I remained in Germany, beguiled by a fresh world emerging from the wreckage.

It wasn't meant to happen, but I fell in love with the German girl. Considering that our two nations had waged a brutal war for five years, it was astonishing that Friede and I even liked each other, let alone grew into lovers.

Before I met Friede, my knowledge of Germany was based upon propaganda posters and newsreels displaying an endless sea of jackboots flooding across Europe. I was convinced that Germans were evil and sinister after witnessing the results of the Nazis' scorched-earth policy in Holland.

My black-and-white opinions about Germany changed when I crossed through their borders and encountered a civilisation turned into a wasteland by aerial bombardment. On the ground, I witnessed emaciated German children living in appalling conditions in the ruins of their city. It was at that moment I accepted that both the damned and the innocent suffered in this war. The longer I stayed in Germany, the more I understood that Friede was both my Beatrice and my Virgil. She was the one who was to lead me through Germany's post-war inferno and perhaps towards our own paradise.

Friede was an excellent guide through both present-day Germany and her country's recent past, but sometimes the maps were filled with errors created by the imperfections and the prejudice of the cartographers. There were moments when Friede expressed an overwhelming shame and guilt for the crimes of her elders, but at other times she couldn't fully digest the totality of Germany's barbarity under Hitler.

Friede said it was impossible to fully comprehend the ever-expanding list of heinous acts her country had committed. She compared it to a child having a father who is wonderful to his own family, but is found guilty of murdering many people in the neighbourhood.

'You think to yourself; was this the same man that loved me and fed me and cared for me; yet did all of these wicked things to our neighbours?'

In many ways, Friede was just an ordinary teenager savouring the liberties of youth, discovering the pleasures of sex and the exhilaration of being adored and wanted by men.

'I love the way you look at me when I wear that summer dress with my new white shoes.'

Friede was nonchalant about male and female relationships and casually warned me that she saw other men.

'There are other boys, you know,' she said in a carefree whisper one day.

'Oh?' I responded, acting as if I were cosmopolitan and blasé.

'Like you, they take me on walks or to a café,' she added.

'Who are they? Anyone I know?' I asked suspiciously.

'Of course you don't know them. One is a German boy who I have known since I was four. And the other one is a Tommy who likes to talk to me.'

I bet he does, I thought cynically.

Friede absorbed my silence and tried to explain her feelings about me and the other young men in her life. She said that her whole world had changed the day the war ended. Peace was difficult, hungry, and complicated, but it was also exhilarating. She wanted to enjoy the simple pleasure of being alive and young with few restrictions.

'Harry, you must take things slowly with me. Let our hearts grow for each other as we explore this new world,' she told me, skipping slightly ahead of me.

'Sure,' I said, 'you're right.' And then I lied. 'You know I'm seeing other German girls, so don't get too comfortable with me, if you know what I mean.'

I was no actor and my shoulders stooped and my face displayed a painful heartache. Friede noticed and became more serious.

'Those other boys are nothing to me. I am very fond of you. You are so ... what is the word ... gallant? I am very grateful to you. I just don't know yet what we will become, friends or lovers. So don't be cross, please understand.' Friede added: 'I shall always be your comrade. My heart will tell me when it is time to give it to you or another. Now stop pouting,' she admonished me. 'Buy me some flowers before you walk me home.'

Friede introduced me to her past like I was the Sultan in *Scheherazade*; there was a story every night that never finished and led further into her soul. She revealed her illegitimacy to me, her experience as a foster child and evacuee. She was adamant that if we were to continue seeing each other, she wanted 'No dark places in your heart, no jealousy, and no anger in your soul. Between us, Harry, things have to be light as a Strauss operetta or as fun as the jitterbug.'

Tentatively, we began to learn about each other's likes and dislikes to see if we shared anything in common, except surviving a war from opposite sides.

'I love to read poetry,' I told her.

'Wordsworth, he is a good poet, but Goethe is more universal,' she responded.

'I've never heard of Schiller, but everyone in the world knows Shakespeare.'

'Shirley Temple, I loved the way she could dance.'

'What about Harold Lloyd?'

'I don't know him, but you must know Dick und Dorf?'

'Who are they?'

'You know, the fat and the thin man, who wear the bowler hats.'

'You mean Laurel and Hardy.'

'That's right, Dick und Dorf.'

During our first few weeks together, Friede and I didn't

have much physical contact, except we held hands on occasion. Sometimes she even let me kiss her lightly on the lips or play with her hair. I would sometimes catch her staring deep into my eyes, trying to decipher what was greater, my lust or my affection for her.

Friede wasn't a patriot, but she was proud to be German. She knew her country's history and achievements in music, philosophy, art, and the sciences. Friede also admitted that Germany's character, its national greatness, was also the ember that sparked its evil. On one of our many walks, we strolled down an avenue showered in dust and demolition. Friede pointed to a group of women working outside their apartment block.

'Look at them, they have nothing and yet they will still sweep their stoop. They will always make sure the inside of their homes are clean. Even if they have no food to eat, Germans will always make sure they are dignified and clean. It is what we learn from birth. It doesn't matter if you are poor or rich, you must have discipline and pride in yourself.' Sadly, she added: 'This is what led us to this Gomorrah. Our discipline transformed us into criminals.'

On another day, we were drinking wine at an outdoor river café, when she told me: 'I think my emotions were created in the social clubs of Weimar Germany because they are so democratic, so contradictory. I am up and down and all over the map.'

'You seem all right to me,' I replied.

Friede shook her head. 'No, I have so many anxieties. I am afraid a lot of times, for no real reason. It is a gift from the Nazis.'

Friede explained that she was nervous and self-conscious because of her illegitimacy. She was confused by where and to whom she belonged. Was it with her mother or her foster parents? Did any of them really want her or even love her? She was afraid that people judged her because her mother took a rich lover and her biological father was a socialist.

'That is why I read so many books,' she explained. 'I am looking for another character that might resemble me or my life, even if they are just fiction.'

I confessed to Friede that I had the same fantasy as a boy and would hunt through novels looking for my identity or the cause of my family's misfortunes.

'Did you find anyone who was like you?' she asked.

'No, I'm afraid I have only found escape from the people around me. What are your favourite books?' I asked.

'Too numerous to count,' she replied. 'Many of them were forbidden under Hitler because they were considered anti-German. They even called Thomas Mann 'an enemy of the people'. But Mutti still had a copy of *Buddenbrooks*, which she let me read. There were no books at my foster parents' house. They were simple people and didn't read much, except my foster father liked Karl May to drown out my foster mother's complaints.'

'So you and your mother were anti-Nazi then?' I asked.

She looked at me with dark impenetrable eyes and said: 'Before the war, everyone was pro-Nazi, even if they had doubts about Hitler. Now everyone is anti-Nazi, even if they have doubts about the British and Americans. My family survived like everyone else did in Germany. We had two faces: one for the world in black uniforms and another for life behind closed doors. You know,' she added conspiratorially, 'my mother even joined the Nazi party.'

'What?'

'Yes, it's true. Her lover Henry said it was good for his business; it probably was, considering he imported and sold tobacco products. Henry joined the party in 1939 because it was easier to sell lighters and humidors to officers' clubs if you could say you were a member of the party. My mother became a member of the Nazi party in 1942. It was a simple decision for her. Too many people were asking questions about me because I lived with a foster family and she lived with a much older businessman. There was always someone sticking their nose into our business and asking about my real father, Fritz. Funny how people stopped gossiping once she got her party badge.'

Friede's illegitimacy tortured her. Being a bastard dug a deep furrow inside of her personality. It made Friede believe she wasn't complete, that her existence was evidence for a crime of passion. She believed she was just the product of a love affair that ended in shame.

'It is a stain on the child more than on the parents,' she said bitterly. 'Children made fun of me because I didn't have a father. I didn't fit in because of my mother's avant-garde lifestyle and my polar-opposite life with my foster parents. Mutti's way of life made it hard for me to make friends. But even the lone wolf sometimes wants to be liked. So at school, I was a good National Socialist and said "Sieg heil" with the rest of my classmates.' She paused and then continued. 'Why do you look at me like I just said I followed the devil?'

'Did you believe in Hitler?' I asked.

'What a silly question. When Hitler came to power in 1933, I was five. I was too young for politics. I only knew what adults told me, or what I heard on the wireless and saw at the movies or at school. We were taught: "The Nazi party saved us from anarchy." So yes, I believed in Hitler because I believed in my mother and my foster parents and my teachers. Once, I even told my class that I met Hitler in Berchtesgaden on summer holiday.'

'Did you?'

Friede looked at me as if I was a simpleton and said, 'Sure, and he shook my hand! Hardly, I was just trying to impress the class with a fib no one could contradict. If it makes you feel any better, I can tell you I hated the Hitler Youth. But that is because the girls were all bullies in my squad, so I tried to avoid them as much as possible. So,' she added, while looking at her face in a compact mirror, 'is the interrogation over? Am I now de-Nazified enough for you?'

'I'm sorry; I didn't mean to hurt you.'

'You didn't,' she replied, snapping the compact shut. 'I just believe you can't possibly know what it was like to live in Germany under Hitler. No matter what I tell you, you will never understand what it was like, and you will always say underneath your breath, "Us Brits would never act like that." Maybe not, but ask the Irish what they think of jolly old England. I am sure they have a different story to tell. Germany did horrible, unspeakable things to millions of people and we are rightly guilty, but I don't want to talk about it any more because all of it just makes me sick inside.'

In the time it took to change a phonograph, Friede could veer from extreme emotional brooding to playfulness. One evening, we sat on a park bench and argued whether occupying soldiers behaved no better than the Wehrmacht in France. Fed up with the conversation, she grabbed a box of matches that was resting on my cigarette pack. She struck a handful of matches and tossed them at me to see how I would react. Of course, I returned fire. Neither of us blinked in this game of combustible chicken. The competition ended only when the box was empty of flaming projectiles.

At other moments, Friede was guilt-ridden by the wretched circumstances faced by refugees. When we encountered a group of them slumped on the street, Friede took a fruit basket I had purloined from RAF stores and handed it out to them.

'They need it more than me or my family. Look at them; they must have travelled all the way from Lithuania. What is going to become of them? Who will help them?' she pleaded.

She began to hand out apples and pears to the displaced family. It looked to me like all the kindness in the world wasn't going to save them from annihilation. Caustically, she said, 'You take everything from us, you English, and you think we should be grateful like a dog because you are a better master than Hitler.'

I watched her feed the refugee family until there was nothing left to give. With the basket empty, she dropped it to the ground and swept their youngest child into her arms. 'If only there were more people like us, there would be no war, no Hitler, no Stalin, and no hunger.'

CHAPTER 4

A coffee house
on the banks of ruin

When August came, the residents of Hamburg sweltered within the skeleton of their defeated city. Record temperatures scorched the northern hemisphere and the city's ruins were bleached white by the sun, while at night a crisp desolate breeze floated in from the Baltic.

In the dwindling days of summer, Hiroshima and Nagasaki were incinerated by atomic explosions that ended the Second World War in the Pacific. All nations were now at peace with their fellow man. In Germany, it certainly didn't feel like civilisation was in harmony with itself. Europe was divided between the Soviet army and the Allied forces in an uneasy détente. Anarchy and hunger threatened Western Europe. Political grievances, black-market turf wars, and old scores against collaborators were settled at midnight with a loaded revolver. Peace in Europe was as uncomfortable as a suit too small in the shoulders.

While the puppet-masters – the banks, the politicians and the generals – pulled strings behind the scenes and shifted the continent politically and financially, I was being tugged deeper into Friede's world. I orbited her like a faithful satellite, while she tentatively introduced my good character and name to her closer girlfriends. She smuggled me into their conversations and inflated my generosity and kind nature.

'Look what he brought my family, a whole kilo of cheese. He even found me tooth powder to clean my teeth. This Tommy always tries to converse in German, even when he mixes up the words.'

Among her friends, I was becoming known as the Brit who wasn't looking for a quick shag underneath the linden trees. At the beginning of our courtship, I was left to linger in the background. Friede kept me ignorant and oblivious to most of her everyday world. She was still uncertain about the depth or distance our friendship would travel. Friede purposely kept me apart from her friends. She was afraid they might reveal confidences to me about her life or disapprove of her dating a foreign occupier.

In late August, I was introduced to her friend Gerda. The two had been friends since early childhood and it was an alliance built upon trust and protection. Gerda was the first friend Friede made when she was sent to live with her foster parents in Hamburg's working-class district of Altona. Both girls lived in the same apartment block and from the day they met, Gerda acted as her bodyguard against gossips and bullies. Friede's friend was a peroxide blonde who was physically pretty and emotionally and intellectually uncomplicated. Past or future tense meant little to Gerda because she lived without introspection. To her, one day you were born and many years later you died. It was the in-between living that mattered to her.

I took them both out for coffee to a riverbank café in the Blankenese district. It was an area popular with occupying forces because its restaurants still functioned with pre-war efficiency. An old and shuffling maître d' brought us to our table. Friede remarked that the café had been in business since the days of the Kaiser.

'When I was about ten, my mother and her boyfriend Henry brought me here. It was filled with stuffy Nazis. I see the uniforms are different, but the cakes remain the same.'

'Hush, Friede,' said Gerda. 'I have never been here, so it is all new for me.'

It was a beautiful outdoor restaurant for a well-to-do crowd. Money, not ideology, was its political stripe. That was why it survived the Kaiser's abdication, the assassination of democracy, and Hitler's bloody end. Regardless of who was in power, the menu at the café remained the same: Vienna coffee, Sachertorte, and VSOP brandy. The café welcomed occupation as it did every historical event: with a cash-only policy.

It was a warm, cloudless day and the restaurant tables were crowded with loud British troops and their female companions. It looked like there was an equal portion of officers and enlisted men chatting and flirting with young German women. Although the occupation command frowned upon fraternisation, it was almost impossible to enforce. The occupiers were young men at the peak of their rutting age and had endured five years of war, privation, and the threat of obliteration. So, irrespective of HQ's fear that contact with the civilian population would lead to an outbreak of venereal disease, corruption in the ranks, and a diminished capacity to keep order in Germany, nothing was ever really done to implement the regulation.

The atmosphere at the café was as carefree as if it were a summer's day before the war. But that was because everyone was facing the river. No one dared turn towards Hamburg's skyline, where it was Gomorrah, the day after Lot had packed up and left. Hamburg was no more than a putrefying animal body where maggots and carrion fed off its carcass. Underneath the city's mountains of ash, cement, bricks, and burned beams were the mummified corpses of some 30,000 bombing victims. They had perished during the RAF firebombing raids in July 1943.

'Last year, you could still smell it,' Friede noted while she put on fashionable sunglasses and got comfortable in her chair.

'Smell what?' I asked, while her friend Gerda looked out towards the river, uninterested.

'The stench from decaying bodies trapped underneath the city's wreckage,' she replied. 'Last summer, you needed to place a handkerchief sprinkled with eau de cologne against your face to stop the odour of rotting flesh from getting into your nostrils. It was overpowering. Even in the winter of 1944, how do you say, the taste, is that the right word? The taste of death overpowered winter's frigidness. Hamburg is a tomb,' she concluded morbidly.

The waiter arrived and set down our order at the table. He was dressed in an immaculate white coat, black tie, and dark trousers. He bowed and scraped before me and fawned over the two women. Contemptuously, I imagined he had displayed the same amount of servility when his customers had been Gestapo officers with their dates.

I offered the ladies a cigarette from my Player's pack,

which they both hungrily accepted. I placed my cigarettes on the table. With Hollywood gallantry, I lit our cigarettes. I was about to bring the match to my smoke when Friede suddenly blew it out.

'Don't forget, it is bad luck being the third one to be lit.'

'I don't think we have to worry about snipers any more. Do we?'

Gerda laughed: 'Both of you should be careful of Cupid; he is the only one who will get you two into trouble.'

Gerda slurped her coffee piled high with fresh cream, while Friede used a spoon to savour each mouthful of rich butter fat. Her friend smiled and laughed at my jokes, even if she couldn't fully understand them. Friede intently observed how I treated Gerda and was obviously making mental notes of whether I was being kind or cruel. For some time, we talked about music. The two women were hungry to know about American singers, swing bands, and whether I had any of their phonographs.

'Do you have Benny Goodman?'

'I adore Tommy Dorsey.'

'What about "Pennsylvania 6-5000"?'

'Glen Miller,' I told them, 'is very popular.'

I suggested we should all go to a dance held at one of the Air Force clubs in the near future: 'We can hear swing music played by some great bands?'

Considering I didn't know how to dance, it was a bold offer, so I quickly changed the subject. I suggested as an alternative that I bring some phonographs over to Friede's mother's apartment. 'We can listen to some good music and make it our own private party.'

'I would still rather go out dancing,' Friede said with disappointment.

The afternoon passed quickly and pleasantly as everyone skirted unsettling incidents from the past or our precarious present. Only once did I let the conversation drift into uncharted waters, when I foolishly asked Gerda if she had any brothers or sisters. Gerda's eyes grew dark. 'Two,' she answered dejectedly. 'I have not seen my brother Erwin since 1942. He was in the Africa campaign. He was taken prisoner by the British. At least he is safe because he is a POW in Britain.' Gerda stopped her narrative and asked, 'Could I have another cigarette? Bitte.'

Her younger brother, Hans, hadn't been as lucky because he had fought on the Eastern front. When I closed the lid of my lighter, she resumed the story. He was at Stalingrad and couldn't endure the brutality. He tried to desert to the Russians. Unfortunately, Hans failed in his attempt to surrender to the Reds. He was caught by his own side, who subjected him to a front-line court martial. Found guilty of cowardice and desertion, Hans was sentenced to death. The verdict was carried out within minutes of the judgement. He was strung up on a telegraph pole, like it was a frontier lynching. A sign was hung around his neck which read: *Coward.*

The waiter arrived with our bill. He presented it on a silver tray that was placed obsequiously before me. He officiously swept the table of crumbs with a shiny brass-handled brush. There was a hasty servility to his movements because other soldiers with their German girls were eager to pay for coffee by the river. I stubbed my cigarette into the ashtray and tried to leave a fat tip on the table, but Friede commented out loud: 'That is just foolish, Harry. That stupid waiter is already rich on Tommy money, better to give him half and we can enjoy the rest somewhere else.'

I picked up part of the gratuity and sheepishly thrust it back into my trouser pocket. When I stood up, I noticed Gerda had hastily gathered up spare sugar cubes from the coffee saucers and put them into her pocket.

The three of us walked along the riverbank. The water was sluggish and covered with a sheen of petrol. The sterns of scuttled naval ships perched themselves above the waterline like markers leading towards the dockyards. Off in the distance, the harbour was still. It was a testament to the air war against the city. The port was now only broken awnings and collapsed steel cranes resting derelict across docking slips. We strolled on a path along the Alster. It was an exquisite walkway decorated with ancient trees and ornate benches. The sky was clear, the sun warm, but there was a dusky smell in the air coming from the ravaged city beyond.

We walked with Gerda to a black market where she could barter cigarettes for sausage. The market was in the ruins of the working-class district, near the docklands. There were rumours; Gerda said that this place had the best rate of exchange between fags and foodstuffs. While we walked, dust blew up from the bomb craters where buildings had once stood. All around me were gaping holes in the cityscape, as if a giant animal had bitten a chunk of flesh from a carcass. In other places, ziggurats of debris formed, where buildings had caved in onto the street. In some spots, a giant bulldozer had brushed ruined neighbourhoods off to the side as one would rake leaves for burning.

Everywhere, there was a loud, monotonous clicking and scraping sound coming from old women pecking through the rubble. They were known as the 'brick Omas' ('Oma' being German for grandma). They scavenged around the wrecked streetscapes looking for salvageable masonry to rebuild the sacrificed city. The old women wore rags and torn aprons over their clothing. Brick dust coated their hair and faces, while their hands were blistered and cut from handling bomb debris that they gathered in neat piles and placed along the roadway. They worked without complaint, reminding me of the Israelites building Pharaoh's necropolis. Sometimes, scores of old women were killed when they tripped an unexploded bomb trapped in the wreckage.

In the background, amid the industrious Omas, lurked a pack of men in various stages of deformity. A man missing a leg hobbled around on a dubious crutch that barely kept him upright. Beside him stood an armless man whose shirtsleeves looked like sails empty of wind. In the group, there were several other men whose heads were wrapped in dirty bandages. These war victims huddled around broken concrete as if waiting for the old women to reclaim them like the other refuse in the street. The uncontaminated scent from my crisp RAF uniform stirred them from their crippled indolence.

'Tommy, cigarette für einen Kameraden.'

'Tommy, chocolate bitte, für meine Kinder.'

'Tommy, Tommy,' went the chorus of maimed men living in the shadows of burnt-out buildings.

We quickened our pace and rushed away from these men. We soon approached the black market where Gerda wished to trade. All around the haphazard, open-air market, thuggish-looking men guarded the perimeter from thieves and the occupying authorities. Generally, the British turned a blind eye to this commerce of survival. However, on occasion, especially if the market was dealing in liquor or medicine, a less than honest bureaucrat, officer or NCO demanded a kick-back to keep the business permit 'official', so to speak.

I bade goodbye to Gerda and uncoordinatedly kissed her cheek. Friede spoke rapidly and lovingly in German to her. When they finished talking, Gerda called out: 'Tschüss, Puppe.'

'I imagine she'll do all right in there,' I said. 'She's quick-witted and no fool. I like her.'

'If anyone wants to live in Germany, they cannot be a fool. As for Gerda, I trust her with my life and would a hundred times over. She would never betray me, or stab me in the back for money, man, or country. Gerda is not complicated, but she is beautiful in her simplicity. I have other friends, who you shall meet, who are different, but I need them just the same to make me complete.'

'What did she just say to you?'

'Oh that,' Friede said, laughing. 'Gerda said, "See ya, doll." We must really begin to work on your German,' she added.

'Doll?' I asked, puzzled.

Impatient and perhaps a little peeved that a part of her private life was being opened up to an outsider, she explained that it was a pet name for her. Friede's mother, out of guilt for making her live with foster parents, bought her daughter expensive clothes. It made the other children who lived in the working-class district think Friede resembled a princess or a doll, fallen on hard times.

CHAPTER 5

The city in the shadow
of the Michel

F riede and I walked back towards the river below the city centre. A wind had picked up and the air smelled of burning rubbish, while soot and ash rained down onto the pavement. This eruption originated from a truck, puffing along and slowing up the thoroughfare in front of us. Its roof was fitted with a boiler and a steam pipe. The vehicle dragged three carriages behind it like a primitive train.

It moved like a rheumatic centipede. A young boy raced across the top of the truck, feeding the boiler with an odd assortment of fuel ranging from chair legs to telegraph poles sawn down to size. The boy, like Vulcan's apprentice, fed the boiler and shifted the burning timber with iron tongs to increase the inferno. The contraption wheezed ahead of us like a castrated dragon let loose on a desolate industrial wasteland, belching smoke, ash and cinder.

'What is the matter?' Friede asked. 'Have you never seen German ingenuity before?'

'It's the strangest thing I have ever encountered.'

Friede explained that when the Nazis began to run out of petrol, cars and lorries were converted to run off coal and scrap wood. Mechanics attached primitive steam engines to Volkswagen motors. They were slow, smelled horrible, and were as dirty as mud. Friede laughed and pointed at the truck painfully meandering up the road and said, 'Look, there goes Germany's secret weapon to win the war.'

Suddenly we were near the harbour, which flowed out to the Elbe River. Apart from the homeless, few people ventured onto this roadway. Ahead of us was a scattering of refugees who carried the weight of their lives on their backs, or pushed it on baby prams with warped, squeaking wheels. I saw a family dragging an enormous clock in their cart, its weights and pulleys clanking and screeching over the bumpy road.

Friede looked at the slim traffic of people and explained: 'The DPs [displaced persons] always seem to take the most ridiculous objects with them on their journey. I don't understand it. Why would you haul around a timepiece? It can only remind you that your day is done.'

'What would you take into exile?' I asked.

Friede thought for a moment and replied: 'My friends, my family, books, a phonograph, and if you are good to me, maybe even you, liebchen. What about you, Tommy, what would you take?'

I smiled and quoted Omar Khayyam: 'A jug of wine, a loaf of bread and thou, beside me. I'd also bundle onto my wagon as much luck as it could hold.'

'You are a brave soul if that is all you need to make you happy in banishment.'

I didn't know where Friede was taking me but I grew concerned by our rapid plunge into the dead flesh of Hamburg. We were approaching the epicentre of the catastrophic 1943 Allied bombing mission, codenamed Operation Gomorrah.

'Are you sure it's safe to be here?' I asked.

'Yes, come on; let's get through this street quickly. Besides, you have a gun in case we get into trouble.'

I had almost forgotten about my weapon; it was a required accoutrement while outside of camp. It was a Sten gun, which I believed put me in more danger from involuntary discharge than any threat from disgruntled former Nazis.

On either side of the road, windowless, lifeless, disintegrating buildings stood ready to crumble into unrecognisable cement. It was like walking through an excavated Pompeii long after Vesuvius had destroyed its citizens. The neighbourhood was bombed into non-existence because of its proximity to the harbour. Only a handful of people survived the firebombing; most were condemned to death by flames, suffocation, or drowning. A conflagration was created by the incendiary bombs. It produced hurricane-strength fire winds that melted people, animals, and inanimate objects as it bellowed across the city, consuming anything and everything that was combustible.

The road abruptly opened up onto a boulevard. Against the destroyed cityscape, a resolute statue of Charlemagne stood. The effigy looked bemused. Its sculpted arm pointed rigidly towards the destruction. Behind him, something else had survived more or less unharmed through those nights of relentless bombing. It had dodged the uncountable bomb tonnage dumped onto this city from Flying Fortresses during the day and Lancasters bombing at night. It alone remained poised, and looked perhaps even nonchalant at its survival. On closer inspection, I could see that parts of the edifice had suffered some bomb damage. However, in comparison to the surrounding wasteland, it appeared unmolested.

Friede pointed and said: 'That is Saint Michael's Kirche. The "Michel" is Hamburg's most famous church. The cathedral is over 400 years old and a testament to Hamburg's greatness as a maritime city. It witnessed our downfall under the Nazis. But we believe that as long as the Michel remains, Hamburg will survive and prosper and its people will rebuild their lives. It is beautiful, isn't it?'

'Yes,' I agreed reluctantly, 'it is very beautiful.'

I had a strained relationship with churches and those in charge of delivering God's word to the ignorant. Belief had long ago been beaten out of me by sexless nuns and alcoholic priests. I suspected that the church survived because it was a reliable geographic beacon for the RAF. It helped guide the waves of bombers onwards to their targets. The cathedral was like a trumpet to the walls of Jericho. Its survival wasn't divine intervention, but military practicality.

'Every Christmas Eve,' Friede continued, 'the Michel's bells rang at midnight. You could hear their chimes from my mother's home in Fuhlsbüttel, ten kilometres away.'

Friede picked up some bomb debris from the ground. Perhaps it was part of a roof or the side of a building; now it was just a shred of mortar. She played with it in her hand as if weighing the consequence of war and wickedness. After some thought, she dropped the small souvenir of wreckage

47

and said, 'I just can't believe in God, at least not God from the Bible.'

'How could he exist? What creator allows all this cruelty to inhabit the Earth? What type of God allows Germany to go mad and kill the Jews? What God lets Spain and Russia slaughter their innocents in civil and class warfare? Who would make a world and walk away from it as if it were a sandcastle on a beach at high tide?'

Friede wiped dirt from her hand and brushed away some hair that had fallen onto her face.

'After all of this waste and destruction what can you believe in, Friede? What can anyone believe in?' I asked.

She looked at me for a moment and after a brief second of reflection, she said: 'I think there is something greater than man. It is not human or divine. It is energy. It came when the universe formed from the void of nothingness. It was like the first spark from a flint. The ember gave humanity conscious life. Our awareness is a gift, but it comes with a price; you only get one turn, one spin at the wheel, and then you are thrown back into the cosmic vapours. There are no second chances. As for eternity, it is unconscious without dreams; the dead are like amoebas floating on the ocean's waves.'

'So there is no heaven?' I asked.

'No, you just walk to the end of your road.'

'What happens then?'

'There is nothing waiting for you at the finish. We just return to particles, lost memories, lost hopes.'

Friede's arms were at her sides and the hem of her skirt rustled in a wind coming off the river.

'Harry, now you look at me like I am crazy,' she said quietly.

She stopped and moved away from me, then threw her head back and stared upwards to the church tower that climbed 130 metres up towards the horizon. She was caught in the rapture of that afternoon.

'If some beauty still exists, life cannot be that bleak. Come on; let's go, before we are late for the train home.' Friede dashed off ahead and left me frozen in my thoughts.

I woke and called out, 'Wait for me!' I jogged to catch up with Friede while the Sten gun bounced against my arm. I was out of breath when I finally reached her on Marseiller Strasse, near the Dammtor train station.

'Tommy, if you want to keep up with me, you should take better care of yourself. At school, I always won the hundred-metre dash because I liked the freedom of being alone, rather than being in a pack of schoolgirls.'

We now walked together towards the Dammtor train station, located across the street from a rollicking armed forces' nightclub called The Victory. The train station was the size of London's St Pancras, but lacked its architectural beauty. The Dammtor was equipped for both inner-city and regional travel. In the early days after the war, its primary importance was as a terminal for inner-city travel. The U-Bahn subway was the only efficient method for people to travel through Hamburg and its suburbs, as petrol was available only for British military vehicles.

We pushed our way through a crowd congregating at the front entrance. Inside, Friede hung on to me as we slid past the queue of people resigned to the new order of things in Germany. The platforms teemed with desperate-looking characters, while overhead pigeons and sparrows swooped and darted through the exposed skylight. Below, civilians were divided into groups of two or three people. Their eyes darted to the ground when they got sight of a British uniform.

Across the platform, the U-Bahn riders scurried to their trains. They dragged unwieldy luggage stuffed with what remained of their pre-war lives. It was now to be traded for food or medicine. On the inner walls of the train station, message boards had been hastily erected. They were crammed with pictures of lost relatives, lovers or friends. Sad notes were tacked up: 'Hans Schumann, I am now at Opa's, your loving Inga.' Miserable pictures were jammed against a dozen other photos. Each snapshot asked to be recognised, remembered, and loved. However, the hot August sun leaked through the station's rafters, blistering the edges of the photos as if to say, 'Don't waste your breath looking for me: I am already dead, my body lies with the nameless that died at the side of the Autobahn.'

Railway employees patrolled the station wearing worn uniforms that looked ready to disintegrate no matter how cleaned or starched they were. Whistles rested threateningly on their lips while passengers diligently looked to follow their orders. Even in defeat, Germans still craved a well-executed command even if it was only to stand ready for an approaching train.

An electrified train entered the station and edged past us. Passengers were pressed up against the windows like guppies in a fishbowl with too little water. When the train screeched to a halt, middle-aged men wearing old homburg hats and soiled overcoats spilled out of the doors. They shuffled out towards the street with their heads bowed as if frightened to look at the ruins around them and the sunlight above them. Behind them, women followed, clutching cloth bags ripe with silverware and wrapped china to be bartered for food.

Small orphaned children darted around the platform searching for discarded cigarette ends. They were bottom-feeders who wore rancid trousers and coal-smeared pullovers as if they were waifs from Victorian London. If they were lucky, they found a handful of partially smoked Capstans or Player's on the dirty platform floor, which were sold for a few pfennigs to teenage gangsters employed by the German mafia. The mob recycled the cigarette stubs with the labour of homeless children and destitute women into new cigarettes of questionable quality, taste, and hygiene. Eventually, the newly fashioned cigarettes ended up in the mouths of indigent Germans who tried to quell the hunger pangs created by the starvation rations thrown to them by the occupation forces.

The rail police blasted their whistles with menace. The order was barked to immediately board the U-Bahn train. Friede and I were herded towards the railway cars. The embarkation resembled a scramble by passengers on a fast-sinking ship with too few lifeboats. We were jostled into the first car by the momentum of the people behind us.

Outside, the police held back disappointed passengers who were too late to board. Inside, I was hit by an overwhelming stench of cabbage and body odour. There was an exhausted gloom painted on the occupants' faces. I had seen the same defeated look on unemployed miners in West Yorkshire during the Great Depression. It was an expression of pain and surprise from a person who couldn't quite work out how they had lost everything at life's roulette table.

It was claustrophobic in the train, but the Germans were either unaware of the lack of oxygen or had grown stoical to the means in which they had to travel around town. Friede said, 'There is more air at the rear of the train.'

We jostled through the crowd of exhausted travellers. A teenage boy, dusty from a day foraging in the wreckage, saluted me. He offered me his seat and an old woman beside him hissed at his gesture.

'Danke,' I said, but offered the wooden seat to Friede, who declined and gave it to a pregnant woman standing nearby instead.

The train entered a tunnel and our car was plunged into darkness while we sped underground below the wrecked city. In lightless obscurity, people coughed nervously, some joked and others whispered as if they were still in a police state. I felt as if I was choking. It was like being trained for chemical attacks by being locked in a cinder-block shed filled with tear gas.

Friede said to me, 'Let's play a game. Come with me.' She grabbed my hand tightly and led me through the standing heaps of people.

'Where are we going?' I asked.

'You'll see. Don't ask too many questions. It spoils the surprise.'

Friede forced us to the compartment door by the front of the train and said, 'The rules to this game are simple, but you will have to learn them while we play.'

'All right,' I agreed with some hesitation.

The U-Bahn squealed into Hallerstrasse station. On a poorly lit subterranean platform, weary passengers waited to board. The door flew open and warm oxygen raced in to fill my lungs. Friede dropped her hand from mine and disappeared out into the station. I froze for a moment. It was difficult to calibrate what had happened. Instinct took over and I jumped out of the carriage. I saw from the corner of my eye that she had run into the next compartment. I took off towards Friede and manoeuvred around passengers and objects. I heard screams from the train guards to halt, which I ignored. I thrust myself into the next compartment and found her grinning at the front of the carriage.

'Next time,' she called out, 'the game gets more difficult. Keep up with me, Tommy, or you are going to lose me.'

'Never,' I said.

With a surge, the train took off. It rattled below the streets, clanking against railway ties, and on occasion the horn screeched. A woman beside us held onto the overhead railing while beads of perspiration trickled down her squat neck. The woman cursed the humidity and someone slid open a widow, which made the compartment as sultry as a rainforest.

While we pulled into the next station, Klosterstern, Friede prepared herself like a runner on a chalk. 'Better keep up this time, Tommy.'

As soon as the door was ajar, Friede darted out and onto

the crowded platform. Energetically, I followed and barged my way through the travellers, who stepped aside as if I was pursuing a criminal rather than playing a schoolyard game. I heard the signalman blow his whistle, which meant the train doors were going to close in seconds. I got nervous, I couldn't find her. I looked in all directions, but couldn't see her through the shuffling phalanx of Germans.

Then, as if the smoke had cleared showing me a pathway, I heard Friede call out to me in her soft accent, making my name sound Arabic. 'Hari,' she cried. There she was frantically waving and jumping, three cars from me.

I cut through the crowd, shouting, 'Schnell, schnell, out of the way.' My Sten gun wrapped around my shoulder jerked and bounced while I sprinted to reach her. The railway guards blew their whistles and the train doors began to close. Just ahead of me, I saw Friede slide into the last compartment. In front of me, an elderly guard blasted the all-clear to the engineer. The doors were now closed to new passengers. I raced up to him and demanded to be let inside the train. The guard tapped his wristwatch to indicate I was too late and out of luck. I screamed so loud the whistle fell from his lips.

'Look, mate, Hitler's kaput. We are in charge now, so open up this bleeding door.'

I saw Friede's head peek up from inside the train and she smiled at my discomfort. Another conductor strode up to me and the elderly guard. He wondered why the all-clear had not been sounded, making the train seconds late for its next stop. The two guards proceeded to argue for several minutes. Finally, the older one relented and allowed me onto the train. I noticed the rest of the occupants eyed me with suspicion and contempt, except for Friede. She rushed up to me and grabbed my hand.

'If you want me, Harry, you have to hold on to me tight or else I will slip away from you, and neither of us wants that, do we?'

CHAPTER 6

Behind the screen door

O ccupied Germany was much like a boarding house in the seaside town of Bridlington: every farce or tragedy was hidden behind closed doors. In Fuhlsbüttel, the people kept schtum and thought it good table manners. Their ability to conceal unpleasant truths was so evolved, a statue of the three wise monkeys wouldn't have been out of place on the main square. The town was adept at ignoring evil, but their true talents lay in doing evil with suburban routine at the local gaol.

Known by locals and inmates as KolaFu (a contraction of Konzentrationslager Fuhlsbüttel), it was constructed in 1911 to house drunks, wife-beaters and swindlers. By the time British forces liberated it on 3 May 1945, it had become a way station for Nazi Germany's undesirables. Many of the region's Jews, gypsies, communists and Jehovah's Witnesses, along with Russian slave labourers, marked time at KolaFu before being dispatched to their deaths at Buchenwald and Ravensbrück.

In the last month of the war, Himmler ordered that the memory of the camp and its prisoners were to be erased from Fuhlsbüttel. On 12 April, the remaining prisoners were marched out of Fuhlsbüttel and north to the port at Kiel. The SS hoped the prisoners of KolaFu might disappear into the Baltic Sea fog.

It was difficult to comprehend that this quiet, bucolic retreat from Hamburg was a willing accomplice to the Holocaust. Barbarity seemed as out of place in Fuhlsbüttel as litter on the streets or untended gardens. Like people who can't remember where they put their keys, Fuhlsbüttel collectively forgot about KolaFu or the prisoners' death march along Langenhorner Chaussee. I did wonder if, on their way to extermination, the prisoners passed Friede's apartment. But much like the first wise monkey, I thought it prudent to hear no evil.

I was now in Friede's company as often as my duties at the airport allowed. We found it difficult to find any privacy for love-making, except on weekday afternoons at her mother's apartment. Intimacy became more complicated for us after the Gellersons, a homeless couple, were allocated a portion of the apartment by the occupying authorities. When Friede's widowed grandfather showed up at their door, the apartment truly became claustrophobic.

'He isn't even my real Opa [grandpa],' Friede said with disdain, 'because my mother is also a bastard.'

'Then who is he?' I asked.

'A miserable old man who says spiteful things about Mutti and me any chance he gets.'

Before one of our afternoon trysts, Friede greeted me on the street with a kiss and said, 'I was getting worried that you wouldn't show. Opa and I have had a terrible row.'

'Nothing could stop me from seeing you,' I told her. 'Look, I brought you some fresh supplies. There is enough meat, veg and wine to last everyone a week.'

'Wonderful, but remember I have to make sure my foster parents get some of the provisions because they can't survive on their rations.'

'I've only got two hands,' I retorted, overwhelmed by her entire family's need for extra food.

'I know it is hard for you to keep pinching stuff from the base, but it is keeping us from becoming beggars on the street. Look, you can see for yourself what good you have done me. The sores on my legs are healing because of the vitamins you got for me.'

When we entered the apartment, a sullen old man greeted me. It was the cuckolded grandfather. He snarled at me in unintelligible German. 'What's up with him?' I asked.

'Oh, he is in one of his moods today. Isn't that right, Opa?' she asked sarcastically.

Friede turned to me and explained: 'He has been on his hobby horse all day. About how everyone is stealing from him. How he never gets enough to eat. Stealing what, I ask? He hasn't had a pfennig to his name since 1913. Before you arrived, he screamed that Mutti and I showed him no respect. We were just illegitimate guttersnipes. I gave the ingrate an earful. I told him he was lucky Mutti let him stay here, considering he chucked her out at twelve years old.

'That is when he got nasty. Isn't that right, Opa? You went on about how the Nazis knew how to do things and wouldn't allow an old man to be treated like rubbish by the daughter of a whore.'

The unshaven old man sat on a wooden stool. He wore thick, uncomfortable woollen trousers held up by bulky braces. He looked as thin and fragile as a tall blade of grass in the dry season. The old man muttered, 'Thunder and lightning.'

'Harry, please give him a cigarette or else we will get no peace.'

I pulled out my cigarette case and offered him a Player's. With shaking hands, he pulled one to his mouth. For a moment, our eyes met; his were filled with watery hatred for everything around him.

'Come,' Friede said. 'Let's get out of the kitchen. I don't know how long we've got until the Gellersons come back. Bring a bottle of wine with you. We'll take it to my room,' she said playfully.

It really wasn't a room, but an alcove that housed a wood-stove and a chaise longue. The walls were thin and covered with heavy floral wallpaper. Along the wall, Friede had pinned up small photos of her girlfriends and glamour shots of German movie stars cut from defunct magazines published during the war.

We put some pillows behind our back and propped our-selves up on the day bed. We drank warm Rhine wine out of a shared coffee cup and ate slices of bread slathered thick with butter. 'Did you hear,' Friede said excitedly, 'the British have started up Radio Hamburg again. So we can finally listen to jazz and dance music banned by the Nazis.'

I laughed and sipped back my wine. I thought these moments with her were the closest to paradise I had ever got in my short and squalid life. Lying beside Friede was like a wish come true from Aladdin's lamp. To me, she was as mysterious as the sphinx and as sensual as nightfall in an exotic garden. I clung tightly to the hope that my desire for her was more than physical want, and that her interest in me went beyond food parcels. Perhaps that was all we could demand from each other after a long war. Maybe the best we both could hope for was the shared warmth from our curled-up bodies and to forget the incinerated city waiting outside.

We finished half a bottle of wine and I sang silly songs. I made extravagant compliments to her eyes, her hair, her body, and her soul. After a while, we undressed each other. We made love on the chaise longue, which was just large enough for us to hold each other tightly, in a selfish and generous longing. For a long time, we remained in Friede's small lair, while outside the thin shuttered door the old man raged against the occupation, his life, and his new lodgings. The din slowly dissipated and faded into the background like a smudge on the wallpaper.

I must have dozed off because I woke to the nakedness of her back and the curve of her spine. I traced my fingers against her skin and noticed that just below Friede's left shoulder she carried a horrible discoloured scar. 'What are you doing back there?' she asked in a sleepy voice.

'Nothing,' I replied nervously as if I had been caught eavesdropping.

'You are staring at my war wound, aren't you?' she asked, turning over to kiss me on my forehead.

'Come on then, give us a cigarette,' Friede demanded, hungry for nicotine. She drew her knees up underneath the blanket and blew a smoke ring from her lit cigarette. 'If you are wondering about the mark on my back, I was in a fire.'

'Did it happen in an air raid?' I asked.

'Nothing so dramatic,' she replied in a matter-of-fact

tone. Friede explained that the Nazis were very big on women being perfect cake- and baby-makers for the Fatherland. At fourteen, Friede was sent by the Hitler Youth organisation to live as a domestic servant with a rich family in Coburg. She was to be taught to be a proper wife, for a proper National Socialist, in a new world where Germany controlled the globe.

Friede giggled as she explained. 'It was a crazy fantasy world created by Himmler and Goebbels. Every girl in Germany was supposed to like a Rhineland maiden who cooked and cleaned and fucked like a rabbit to make blue-eyed, blonde-haired Aryan babies for the Reich.'

Friede laughed and continued her story. She was sent to live with a horrible family who were fanatically pro-Hitler. 'If I didn't clean the silver correctly, the mother scolded me with: "If the Führer was watching you now he would be very disappointed in you, Friede." I think they treated their dog better than me.'

One morning while Friede was making breakfast for the family's youngest son, her back was to the gas stove. She stood too close to the flame and her thick woollen house coat caught fire. The little boy waiting for his meal noticed the smoke rising from Friede's back and screamed, 'Friedl, you are on fire.'

'I was so stupid,' Friede said. 'I panicked and fled, running down the hallway.'

The last thing Friede remembered before blacking out was running down the hall towards a giant mirror. There, she stopped and watched, horrified, as her burning body reflected back into her eyes.

Friede awoke in the hospital with third-degree burns on her back. It was difficult for her to endure the pain because there was no morphine to ease her suffering. The hospital was overwhelmed with victims from a bombing raid that had caused many casualties in Coburg.

Friede said what was worse than the pain were the cries from the near-dead and dying all around her.

'It was horrible. People were crying out, "Jesus save me. God help me, someone please help me." I was so afraid I was going to die in that hospital and the authorities in Hamburg wouldn't give permission for my family to visit me.'

'What about the family you lived with as a domestic?' I asked attentively.

'That stupid family, they came once, maybe twice,' she said harshly. 'The mother wanted to make sure the doctors understood that my injuries were from my own foolishness. You see, they were a good National Socialist family who always took the correct safety precautions. They didn't want any problems from the police because of my accident.'

'It must have been very lonely.'

'It was,' she said with her eyes closed and her back resting on a pillow. 'But there was a nice little boy in the bed beside mine. He called me Edelweiss. His legs were crushed after a building collapsed on him in the bombing. He was very sick, but he was always optimistic and happy, and then one day he said, "Edelweiss, I can't feel my legs." It was gangrene and he was dead the next day,' she finished sadly. 'I don't think he was more than eight.'

'Well, now you know how I got my mark. Later, I will tell you about the time I was evacuated to a farm near

Coburg. I really enjoyed living with that family, but it had its negative side. Their grandfather was a deviant and tried to molest the girl evacuees when they used the outdoor privy.'

Friede crushed her cigarette into a saucer and hastily jumped out of bed. I watched her quickly throw on some clothes.

'You'd better go,' she said. 'Mutti will be back soon. I don't want her to meet you like this, stark naked with a glass of wine in your hands.'

'When will I get to meet your mother?' I asked.

Friede was frantically brushing her shiny hair in front of a tiny mirror hanging from the wall. 'You will meet Mutti on my birthday, which is less than a month away. I can guarantee you on October 20th we will be on our best behaviour and not at each other's throats, like we will be today. Especially if she sees you now, looking like some afternoon Casanova. Come on then, I can hear the Gellersons coming through the door, get up.'

I stood up from the makeshift bed. I picked my uniform off the floor while Friede straightened up her room.

Just before she opened the door and breached the safety of her bedroom, Friede said: 'Before you go, give Opa a few cigarettes; he will be less mean to me when you are gone.'

I followed her out and noticed that the old man had not stirred from the kitchen. Suddenly, the front door opened and the Gellersons entered.

It looked like they had been foraging for supplies because they were carrying potatoes and firewood for the oven. They greeted Friede warmly and ignored both me and the old man.

Before, I left, I handed the old man a half packet of cigarettes. He grumbled, 'Danke schön.' It could have been fuck you, judging by the tone of his voice. I gave Friede a perfunctory peck on the cheek and departed for the base.

It was dusk, but there was still a steady stream of refugees making their way through town. On the way back to camp, I whistled the tune from 'The Teddy Bears' Picnic' and ignored the dispossessed and homeless spawning down the road.

Not far from our camp gates, I stumbled onto a family stalled on the road. Their cadaverous horse refused to drag the family's rickety cart an inch further. It looked like the beast had probably hauled this family and their weighty, useless possessions along the eastern corridor only paces ahead of the Russian army for the past three months. Not only was the cart packed high and wide with furniture; it had the added burden of transporting a couple of toddlers and a young teenage girl. The children looked anaemic, stricken by both terror and extreme hunger, while at the front of the trap, the parents looked equally desolate.

The father cursed the horse as it stood stooped in the middle of a crossroads. He jumped off his wagon and lashed the animal with threats of God's damnation. Froth dripped from the horse's mouth and puddles of foam formed on the cobblestone street below. The man drew a flashing leather whip from his wagon and began to beat the animal. The horse's thin hide was pierced by each lash, while its eyes bulged out of their sockets from pain and hunger.

The blows quickly became too much for the horse; a groan erupted from its mouth. It sounded sad and resigned and it said no more. The horse's bulging eyes turned upwards and watery turds fell exhausted from its backside. Its head twisted up and towards me like a ship before its stern drags the bow to the ocean's depths. The horse's agony was over in seconds. It dropped dead to the ground still shackled to its shuck. Even though the horse weighed nothing, it still brought the cart down on its side. The mother in the front of the wagon and the children at the rear crashed down onto the pavement. The contents of their lives aimlessly spilled from the broken wagon and onto the road.

Crumpled on the side of the road, the mother wailed in indecipherable German. The peasant woman made the sign of the cross, but I thought God had left some time ago for home and no one had taken over his shift.

The father stood over the animal. He looked as per-plexed as a motorist peering under a car bonnet billowing with steam. It was the expression of, 'How could this have happened? I had this car serviced only a month ago.' He dropped the whip and unshackled the horse to right the cart. Then he reloaded the cargo that had fallen across the road. The children climbed onto the back of the cart, the mother sat in the front and continued to gesticulate to Jesus, while the father took the dead horse's place. The man slowly pulled the cart, with his family and the jetsam of their life, away from the crossroads.

The dead horse looked like a pile of old clothes dropped on the cobbled streets. Its lifeless eye stared up into the set-ting sun. Before flies had time to settle on the dead beast, an old woman came out of her house and began cutting into the horse's belly. She yanked out chunks of flesh and threw them into a leather bag.

Others gathered around the old crone and followed her example. They hovered over the horse's corpse with pocket knives or hatchets. They roughly butchered the warm body of the dead animal.

I walked around the famished mob hacking and sawing away and jogged back to camp. The guard on duty at the gate recognised me and said, 'You always come back to camp looking a stone lighter than when you left.'

'One of the many benefits of walking,' I replied.

'As long as you stick to walking and no monkey business, you be all right, Harry.'

'Too right,' I agreed and passed through the gates. Inside, my mind was calculating how to keep Friede and her family alive through the autumn, let alone the winter, on stolen rations.

CHAPTER 7

The bargain between a mother and an uncle

During the last months of 1945, civilian mortality dramatically increased throughout occupied Germany. By October 1945, Hamburg was as desolate as Carthage after Rome laid it to waste. Incessant food shortages, poor sanitation and disease were now as deadly as aerial bombardment to the inhabitants of Hamburg. As if life couldn't get any more miserable for the metropolis, it also suffered from electrical blackouts, water shortages, and a decreasing amount of food rations for its inhabitants.

German society disintegrated into pre-industrial communities ruled by the victorious armies of the West and the East. The occupiers appeared ill-equipped to manage the responsibilities of peace. During the first year of occupation, Germany plunged to the bottom like an elevator with its cables cut. Hamburg existed in the sub-basement of civilisation. Many of its residents lived in hovels dug from the ruins of bombed buildings. It was a miserable time, with starvation and hopelessness driving multitudes of women onto the streets to barter their bodies for cigarettes to battle-numb soldiers.

Hamburg was a city where sexual commerce transpired on every boulevard and beneath every burnt-out street light. When it came to distinguishing between a girl on the game and a girl down on her luck, soldiers were myopic.

The week before her birthday, Friede wanted to introduce me to her foster parents, who lived in the Altona district. We agreed to meet each other in the afternoon at Dammtor station. Unfortunately, I was late for my train and when I arrived I had forgotten where we were supposed to meet. I walked outside, where the glare from the sun temporarily blinded me and left me disoriented in a crowd of strangers. It took me several minutes to adjust to the afternoon brightness, but I finally recognised Friede standing at the entrance to the Victory dance club on the opposite side of the road.

Friede was beside an airman in Canadian uniform. It appeared as if he was arguing with her because several times he threw his hands up, frustrated.

I crossed the street and yelled out, 'Is everything all right?'

Friede looked relieved by my arrival, but the Canadian appeared less so and inquired, 'Who the hell are you? Can't you see I'm talking to this Fräulein? I want to ask her out on a date.'

Friede spoke hastily to me in German: 'This very rude man cornered me and won't let me walk away. He is drunk and stinks of beer.'

I said to the Canadian: 'I think you are a little confused, mate, she's with me.'

'With you?' he asked suspiciously.

I explained to him that we were on our way to meet friends.

'Fuck off,' was his response. 'Give 'em a bit of chocolate or some cigarettes and these Germans will go with you like a stray dog in Cabbage town. They're all fucking tarts.'

'Mind your manners,' I told him. 'If I were you, I'd get on your bike and move on.'

'What ya going to do about it?' he demanded threateningly.

The Canadian swayed drunkenly from one foot to the next and gave me a stare filled with violence and hatred.

I said to him: 'You better hop it or I'm going to bust your head open like a tin of kippers.'

The Canadian was about to take a swing at me, but in the distance I saw a military policeman. I told the drunken airman that the MP was my mate. 'He'll throw you into the glasshouse for disorderly conduct, without looking sideways at you. So best be off home.'

I called out to the MP: 'Oi, George, over here for a second.'

Scared by my bluff, the Canadian tried to run off, but I grabbed his shirt cuff and said, 'Before you go, apologise to the lady.'

'Sorry, miss,' he said in a shallow voice and disappeared into the crowd.

When the MP arrived, he asked what all the commotion was about.

'Nothing, I thought you were my mate's brother. Sorry for the trouble.'

'No bother,' he said. 'This is no place to loiter.' He looked suspiciously over at Friede.

'Is this woman with you?' he asked.

'Yes.'

'Well then, I suggest you both get a move on.'

We walked on and Friede laughed at my deviousness. She gently grabbed hold of my arm and asked, 'When are you going to take me dancing in that club?'

'I'll take you there in a week, when you turn eighteen,' I told her with forced enthusiasm. 'How do we get to your foster parents' apartment from here?'

'Today, we will go through Planten un Blomen. We can take the U-Bahn from there. It is no more than ten minutes,' she said definitively.

Hand in hand, we strolled across the city's botanical park, Planten un Blomen. Even in the autumn, it was a beautiful green space that included an artificial lake populated by graceful swans. Some of the flowerbeds had been turned into potato and cabbage patches, but it was still more picturesque than London's Hyde Park.

It was a quick walk to the U-Bahn station. When we were inside the tube train, Friede gossiped about her girlfriends and how much everyone's lives had changed since the German surrender.

'Gerda for instance is all for having foreign boyfriends. But Ursula wouldn't be caught dead with a Tommy.'

'I don't think we've met,' I said.

'You probably won't. I love her to bits, but she believes shaking hands with a Tommy is something close to treason.'

'What do you think?' I asked jokingly.

Friede paused to collect her thoughts. 'My world has changed for ever. Nobody knows what is going to happen tomorrow or five years from now. Both the war and now this peace have taught me that I am going to experience my adventures today, because nobody can be sure what tomorrow is going to be like.'

When our train passed the Reeperbahn station, Friede spoke in a serious tone of voice. 'I've heard rumours that the British are going to cut our food and wood rations by a third. Do you think that will happen, because I don't know how Mama and Papa are going to be able to survive if their food allotment is reduced? Papa hasn't been able to work since the end of the war.'

I replied, 'Don't worry. I will find a way to take care of them through the winter.'

'That would be fantastic,' she answered in a happy voice.

It would be incredible, I thought, if all my brazen promises to Friede were kept. I calculated that if half of my pledges materialised, everyone would have enough food and fuel to live until the spring thaw. I was terrified that I'd fail and her family's desperate bid to survive was going to end in tragedy. There was only so much I could barter from the mess sergeant or steal from the cookhouse before someone noticed. If I was discovered, my borrowed philanthropy would end with me on charges and Friede out in the cold.

After emerging from the Altona U-Bahn terminal, we went south along the Allee, which had received a lot of bomb damage. The buildings on the street were in a bad state; most were burnt fragments where hungry feral cats and dogs now took shelter. Remarkably, along the way, there were also some apartments and shops that had remained unmolested by the bombing.

'It looks like a lot of people were bombed out here,' I remarked.

'Thousands,' Friede commented in a faraway voice. 'Mama and Papa were lucky. Our building never suffered a direct hit. But I spent a lot of nights in the bomb shelter because we are so close to the harbour. The RAF never seemed to tire from dropping bombs on us.'

Friede asked me if I had ever been in an air raid. When I told her no, she sarcastically responded, 'Of course not, you are in the RAF. Your job was to drop the bombs.'

'Not me,' I said. 'You know I was on the ground in the mobile communications unit.'

'I do,' she responded in a softer tone of voice. 'That is why you are my boyfriend. I would never have a lover who dropped bombs on Germany.'

Ambivalently I nodded, but I wasn't about to condemn my RAF for the brutality of the air war. I knew there were two sides to this conflict and the skippers and crew of Bomber Command suffered appalling casualties. Those men waged a war they didn't create but were compelled to win for civilisation's sake.

I also understood it was just too difficult for Friede or anyone else who had endured the firebombing to be reminded of General Sheridan's aphorism that war is hell.

When we approached her foster parents' apartment on Klausstrasse, Friede pointed towards a five-storey apartment building on the corner. For a working-class apartment block, it seemed stunning and elegant to me. The windows facing down onto the street were immense and although the paint was faded and chipped in places from the masonry, it was an impressive building for the common man.

'This was my home when I was a little girl,' she noted with some ambivalence.

'What about your mother's apartment?'

'That was my weekend home, but only if Uncle Henry said it was OK to go and visit. That is why I always feel like I am just a temporary lodger at Mutti's. At Mama and Papa's, I was happy.' She paused and qualified her statement. 'Well, I felt happiest here, when Mama was nice to Papa and didn't call him all manner of names. Do you see the window beside the balcony on the fourth floor?'

I looked up at the apartment window where Friede had been sent to live in the summer of 1932. The day Friede went to live with the Bornholts, her mother had treated it as a normal outing. 'Mutti packed my suitcase and said, "Hold onto your doll, kid, hold onto your doll."'

Friede wasn't aware that when she left her mother's apartment on Weidenallee, it was for the last time. On the way to her new home in the taxi, Maria Edelmann prepared her daughter for their separation. Maria told her that she would be in the care of the Bornholts for only a short while. It was to let her mother get back on her feet financially. She said there was nothing to worry about because the Bornholts were the kindest of folk and everything was going to work out just fine.

When mother and daughter arrived at the Bornholts' apartment, Maria Edelmann rang the doorbell and kissed Friede on the forehead. Maria said to her daughter:

'Remember to be a good girl for your Mutti and always obey the Bornholts.'

The door opened and Max Bornholt and his wife walked out to greet Friede. Maria Edelmann refused to display any sorrow or any guilt she carried for relinquishing her daughter, and turned emotionally to ice. She let go of Friede's hand and bid her a perfunctory adieu. Maria didn't look back and she didn't cry out her daughter's name when she rushed downstairs to her taxi, which was waiting to take her to her lover's home in the suburbs.

Friede said: 'After Mutti left, Frau Bornholt grabbed me and scooped me inside the apartment. I cried for a week and thought I must have done something very bad to Mutti to be left with the Bornholts.'

'That sounds horrible,' I said.

'That was life in Germany during the Depression. What can you do but survive?' Friede said in a matter-of-fact voice.

Friede explained that the trauma of being separated from her mother quickly passed. 'Soon after Mutti left me with the Bornholts the whole neighbourhood was turned into a battleground between Hitler's Brownshirts and the communists.'

It was called the Bloody Sunday massacre of 1932. In that year, the Nazis were a strong political force, but not a supreme power in German politics. The communist party was one of their major rivals and it had a strong following in working-class districts of Hamburg. The radical SA or Brownshirt wing of the Nazis was entrusted with eradicating their Red rivals once and for all, in the Altona district where Friede's foster parents lived.

So on a seemingly quiet and normal Sunday in July, a street war erupted between well-armed SA stormtroopers and the out-gunned but enthusiastic adherents to socialism and communism. The SA hunted down their Red enemies from apartment block to apartment block and rooftop to rooftop. From her bedroom window, Friede witnessed Brownshirts battle Red-shirts with pistols and machine guns.

'So after all that bloodshed,' Friede said, 'I adapted to living with the Bornholts and Mutti visited me on most weekends.'

I was still confused and asked why the Bornholts were chosen to take care of her.

Friede explained to me that there was no other possible solution for her mother but to have Friede live with the Bornholts because her father Fritz was out of work and out of luck. 'He didn't even live with us,' she said. 'He was like a sailor that rolled in and out of our lives to escape a storm.'

Friede's mother loved Fritz, but she knew their affair was doomed. Ever since he was traumatised by his experiences in the German army in the First World War, Fritz had problems keeping a job. After Germany plunged further into economic and political chaos after the Wall Street Crash, life only became more difficult for him. He wasn't any help to himself and he was certainly no real help to Maria Edelmann. So Fritz moved on and out of Hamburg with a promise to make things right for his daughter and Maria.

Maria Edelmann didn't put much stock in the words of men, especially sentimental ones damaged in the war. She knew Fritz wasn't going to save anyone. The only thing that was going to keep Maria Edelmann above water was her sex appeal to certain men of influence and wealth.

'My mother wasn't going to let me starve. In those days, she was very beautiful and was a gifted singer and dancer. She did what was necessary; Mutti took a rich, fat old man as her lover. His name was Hinrich Karp, or as he used to say: "Friede, think of me as Uncle Henry." Uncle Henry liked me, but he liked me best from a distance. He didn't want me in their Fuhlsbüttel love nest because he was a businessman and some big shot in business and politics. So I was sent to live here with the Bornholts.'

'So your mother chose Hinrich over you?'

'No, it wasn't like that at all,' she said, irritated. 'Back then, Germany was economically destroyed, just like it is today. How could we have survived if Mutti had not become Henry's lover? Do you know?'

'I'm sorry, I don't know.'

'It would have been the orphanage for me and the street for Mutti.'

'But why were you sent to live with these people rather than another family?' I asked. 'Surely, if your mother couldn't provide for you, the government would have sent you to a foster home?'

Friede laughed and explained to me that Hinrich Karp was a man of some influence and authority. Karp also knew that Maria Edelmann wasn't prepared to forsake her daughter for him and the safety he provided. It was imperative that Friede be given a good upbringing and that she was never allowed to forget her real mother or the sacrifices she made for her daughter.

Placing Friede in the care of Max Bornholt and his wife was the best solution for Henry because he knew Bornholt through his import and export business. Bornholt worked for the state railway company in the customs department. He always ensured that Henry got his goods on time with little trouble or government interference. Naturally, for his ability to make Karp's customs problems disappear, Max was rewarded with gifts of cash.

'What did Henry import?' I asked.

'Tobacco, cigars, smoking accessories from lighters to hookahs; he manufactured them or imported them with his partner, Jons Rodmann. Their company, Rodmann und Karp, were known all across northern Germany for good cigars, excellent carved pipes, and elegant silver lighters. How Henry got his goods I was never told, but I am sure there was some dirty business in it. Anyway, you are letting me get away from how I ended up as the Bornholts' foster child.'

Friede told me that Max and his wife Anna weren't happily married. They already had two children, Alvin and Herma, but they were pretty well grown. After their daughter Herma was born, Anna couldn't have any more children. She developed an early menopause, which she blamed on Max's wandering eye for the ladies. Both she and Max thought they might be able to find peace with each other if they could have another child.

So, fortune in the guise of corpulent Hinrich Karp walked into their lives and left Max with an exciting proposal. One typical business day, Karp showed up to Max's office at the railway company to enquire about some tobacco orders held in customs. However, Karp wasn't his usual jovial self and was in a sour mood. So out of sorts was Karp that he began to complain to Max about his mistress's kid, Elfriede.

Henry said: 'The little so-and-so is getting in the way and being a real chatterbox.'

Max, half-serious, said that he would love to make this problem go away for Henry. He even offered to raise the girl like she was his own. Naturally, whether it was his own or someone else's, there were costs involved with raising a little girl.

'Naturally,' said Henry, 'and how many Reichsmarks will this cost me?'

'That many Reichsmarks,' Max suggested, and both men agreed upon a sum to ensure the health and well-being of Elfriede.

The crisis of where to put Friede was solved like it was a problem about what to do with a pet dog that was too noisy. After Friede had related to me how she ended up in the care of the Bornholts, she added with no apparent bitterness: 'Somehow it is funny to me to think how I was traded from one household to the next and everyone said they loved me the more for it.'

'How is that funny?' I asked.

'Well, everyone ended up happy, just like a fairytale. Mama and Papa got a little child to love and some extra money, while Henry got my mother all to himself.'

'And what did you get from it?' I asked.

She smiled enigmatically. 'I got to survive and was loved. That is more than most people ended up with in this war.'

CHAPTER 8

Altona gypsies hide their secrets

We stood outside her foster parents' apartment building on Klausstrasse and I asked, 'Shouldn't we go in?'

'No, not yet,' said Friede. She then grabbed my hand and dragged me across the street and into an alleyway.

'We still have time to see something else,' she said and kissed me.

'I like this part of the tour,' I replied.

'Harry, if you just listen to me for a moment longer, you will know more about me than any other boy I have dated.'

I grew quiet and allowed Friede to lead me further into her world. Friede said that as a very small girl, she played in the abandoned wood behind the alleyway. Being seven, she thought it was a magical place, populated with trolls, wizards, and wonderful secrets. To her, it was like the world found in *Through the Looking-Glass.*

The day I saw it, the spell had definitely worn off because it was now a wasteland and a dumping ground for bomb refuse. It was a much different place during Friede's childhood. Back then, it was a wood where gypsies set up camp and lived in their painted caravans. Friede became friends with a gypsy family and played with their two children. However, when her foster mother found out about her new friendships, she was forbidden to play in the woods or associate with the gypsies. But Friede ignored her foster mother's demand and continued to play with the children from the wood.

'What happened?' I asked.

'Nothing happened to me. But later on, the Gestapo rounded them up and sent them to a concentration camp. Naturally, Mama lied to me and said, "Gypsies are like that, they are never in one place for a long time because they are nomads." It was best to forget about them and have friendships with good German boys and girls.'

Some time after the gypsies had been taken, a neighbourhood boy found Friede playing in the abandoned wood. He asked her what she was doing there. Friede said she was looking to see if her gypsy friends had returned from their trip. The boy laughed and told her the Gestapo had arrested them.

'How could he have witnessed that?' I asked.

Friede answered: 'He said he hid in the bushes and watched them being rounded up, but he was a strange and sinister boy. He warned me about playing alone here and said, "Make sure they don't mistake you for a gypsy, or they will take you next. It will be like you never existed because everyone knows you have no mother or father."'

Friede pulled me away from the ruined wood. We went back up through the alleyway and she remarked that a lot of people she knew disappeared while she was growing up.

'One day they were here, the next day gone and no one said a word. Up the street, there was a sweetshop. It was my favourite shop. It was popular with all of the neighbourhood kids because the lady who owned it was very nice and always gave out free sweets. One day, we were told not to shop there.'

'Why?'

'They were Jews and Mama said the police would give us trouble if we shopped there again. Even my doctor disappeared; he used to let me ride on the side board of his car as he drove to visit patients. He was really a wonderful, kind man,' Friede said, her voice breaking.

'As a child, it was hard for me to understand that people simply vanish from the landscape and disappear into the night. It is impossible to comprehend, especially if every adult refuses to tell you where they have all gone to.'

Friede stood on the street corner, as distant to me as a ship out at sea caught in a tempest. I went to touch her shoulder, but she shrugged off my ignorant empathy. 'Well, well,' she said. 'I am seventeen, alive, and German. I feel guilty sometimes for feeling happiness. I can't bear to think what happened to my gypsy friends. I don't think things ended well for them or for my doctor or for millions of other people. Let's go; Mama and Papa will be wondering where I got to. Don't tell her I was playing in the memory of the gypsies,' she warned.

There was no lift in the apartment block so we had to climb four steep flights of stairs. Waiting for us at the top of the landing were Max and Anna Bornholt. Friede's foster father gingerly approached and enthusiastically shook my hand. The foster mother was more reticent and more rotund than Max. She emanated a cold suspicion for me. It didn't appear to be motherly concern for her foster child, more a condition of her personality that distrusted happiness or good fortune.

After kissing me on both cheeks, Friede's foster mother indelicately thrust me into their large apartment, which was spartanly furnished. At the entrance, their daughter Herma stood beside her young son Uwe. I was barely acknowledged, but her greeting to Friede was frozen in disdain. Herma was eight years older than Friede. Many considered her intensely beautiful, but I didn't see it. To me, Herma wore her good looks like a crown of thorns. Whatever outward beauty she possessed was poisoned by her vile and vengeful temperament. She didn't hide her jealousy towards Friede, nor conceal her contempt towards her father, Max. She despised him for adding another daughter to their household. Herma uninterestedly shook my hand and exhaled an atmosphere of black gloom all around the living room.

'Take my chair,' said Max.

His wife interrupted. 'I am sorry, my husband is slow when it comes to good manners, he should have offered you a seat immediately.'

Friede tried to calm down her foster mother and Herma. 'Mama, let's go into the kitchen so I can show you all the wonderful supplies Harry has brought you.'

It didn't last long and the women began to argue about something I had failed to bring. Max smiled and said, 'Women – they are always happiest when they have something to complain about.'

I reluctantly agreed and tried to converse with him.

'It's a warm autumn.'

'I have experienced warmer.'

'I hope the winter will be mild.'

'It will never be as cold as Siberia,' responded Max. He tapped a deep scar at the top of his left forehead with his index finger and added, 'From the last war. I fought in Russia with the Kaiser's army. A Russian sniper shot me in Galicia. My mates left me for dead, but I was saved by a Russian surgeon who patched up my noggin. I think the doctor fixed me up as good as new. Except in the evenings – I get some fearsome headaches, but that could be from my wife yelling at me.'

Max was bald and wore a suit that was much like him: it had seen better days. He was a relic from another time like my father or my grandparents. I looked at my watch and wondered what was keeping Friede in the kitchen.

He suddenly leaned close to me. 'You speak quite good German.'

'Friede helps me a lot with my pronunciation,' I explained.

'But I don't think you understand Germans,' he added mysteriously.

I offered him a cigarette.

'Normally I don't, but this time, like an old soldier, I will smoke with you.'

He lit his cigarette with a lighter plated with gold.

He saw me admire it and said, 'A gift from Hinrich Karp, Maria Edelmann's lover.'

He handed me the lighter and I played with it while he spoke.

'You know I have been to many places in the world,

first as a soldier, and then as a Reichsbahn employee. It is great fun to travel. When I was young, I had love affairs and girlfriends in many different cities across Germany. What wonderful carefree days they were for me, with so many happy memories for me now. I hope you have had similar experiences in your travels. However, I trust you don't think Friedl is just a bit of fun in a foreign port. I would hate to see her used or hurt by anyone.'

'I would never hurt her,' I told him.

'Good,' Max remarked, inhaling his cigarette.

Max resembled a tired old alley cat sitting on the sofa, who still had enough life in him to pounce at the first sight of a mouse. He looked over to the open window and resumed speaking.

'Friede's had a complicated life, which has been far from ordinary or normal. I love her more than my real daughter. I think I love her more than any person in this world because she was so fragile when she came to live with us. I have tried to make her feel safe and loved. But I don't know if she understands. I am afraid Friede doesn't know where she belongs: with me, with her real mother, or with her real father. Her life is a tangled ball of wool because all the adults in her life have had their own problems and ignored hers.'

'Like what?' I asked.

'Her real father Fritz Adelt was a bit of a dreamer whose spirit was damaged in the Great War. Fritz high-tailed it out of Hamburg after Friede was born. It was hard for him to make a living and with the responsibility of fatherhood, he felt like a man on a ledge. So whether he jumped or was pushed, Fritz deserted Friede and her mother. He left them high and dry. Maybe he had another family, I don't know. What I do know is he didn't have any real contact with his daughter, until it was too late. When your father abandons you for whatever reason, it will haunt the child throughout their whole life. I hope I was a good substitute, but I probably wasn't.'

'Friede has told me that you are the only man she loves as a father.'

Max smiled and said, 'Well, at least I was a better father to her than fat Henry. He couldn't abide Friede when she was small. However, when she grew into a beautiful teenager, Hinrich thought she was just swell. I shouldn't speak ill about Hinrich; he had his moments. At least Hinrich paid me on time, for keeping Friede. Not that there is anything now to show for it. Hinrich was good to Friede's mother when times were good: he always kept her in style. But he was too much of a Nazi opportunist for my liking, but I am not a political man.'

'What do you mean, Nazi opportunist?' I asked.

'Hinrich Karp was a big shot, or pretended to be because it was good for business. If there was money in communism, he'd have quoted Marx instead of Goebbels. But how much he believed in National Socialism is anyone's guess. Nazi lackey or not, Hinrich used his influence sometimes for good and sometimes for bad. For instance, before the war, some meddling Nazi began snooping around questioning Friede's lineage. The party had their doubts about Friede.'

'Doubts? What are you talking about?'

Max leaned forward, and using his fingers to count he replied: 'One: Friede's mother is a bastard. Two: Friede is a bastard. Three: there were rumours about Jews and communists being in on her father's side of the family. Myself, I don't think there was anything to them, but there was some sort of investigation in 1938. I think Henry pulled some strings and people stopped asking questions.'

'Is Friede Jewish?' I asked, dumbfounded.

'Who knows,' he said, raising his hands up towards the ceiling. 'In Germany, only a fool goes digging for the truth. It is best to live in the present. The past is dead and buried. Let it rest in peace. Whatever the truth is, Friede's vagabond life has made her emotionally fragile. She may pretend on the outside that she is strong and hard. However, on the inside, she is frightened. Elfriede doesn't know who she is as a person, as a German, as a human being, because of her family. She needs a fresh start to make herself into the woman she deserves to be. So, I beg you, please treat her gently. She doesn't deserve any more hurt. God knows I have loved her like a daughter, but that is not enough when you don't know who you are and where you came from.'

CHAPTER 9

Life observed from binoculars

By the end of October, our Indian summer had retreated against a cold wind blowing down from the Baltic. As the days grew shorter and the afternoon sky dimmed, the bread lines remained pregnant with refugees and German nationals. In the parks, there was the clandestine sound of handsaws as Germans felled trees and cut them into logs to burn in their wood stoves. There were others like Maria Edelmann who kept their apartments warm with stray coal scrounged from alongside the railway tracks that crossed the city.

Inside the confines of our Air Force base, it was warm and snug. We were well fed and the airport was often somnolent. Scuttled Luftwaffe fighter planes sprouted around the edges of the landing zone with their noses dug into the ground like discarded cigarettes. My mates and I posed for photos beside their rusting fuselages as if we were big game hunters standing near the corpse of an elephant.

Behind the landing zone, a concrete observation tower had been erected by the German aviation league in the 1930s. The five-storey monolith housed the airport's telephone exchange system, RAF regional headquarters, and at the top of the building the air traffic control bridge.

My primary responsibility for the RAF was as a telephone switchboard operator. However, on Saturdays, I was seconded to air traffic control and worked from the observation nest.

The shift was six hours long and unless I brought a book, it was about as exciting as listening to a leaking tap.

On the weekend of Friede's birthday, I scanned the autumn clouds like Gordon of Khartoum looking for relief to arrive. On my watch, it was rare for the drone of approaching aircraft to break the monotony of exposed grey sky. That day proved to be lucky for me, and my headsets crackled with static and a voice from above.

In the distance, I saw a Lancaster approach the aero-drome. I responded to the call in a bored and lazy fashion. My landing instructions were simple: if the strip was empty of lorries, pedestrians or errant cows, use it.

I observed the airmen dismount from their aircraft. They looked as bored as a group of bus conductors because they were now pilots on a milk run. There was no excite-ment or thrill or threats of death except through thrombosis. They walked over to the operations room and surrendered their cargo, which appeared to be condensed milk, mail and spanners. It occurred to me that the Air Ministry might have requisitioned the wrenches to reassemble Hamburg as if it were a broken Meccano toy.

From the air traffic control tower, I was able to see the entire town of Fuhlsbüttel – and nothing ever looked out of place. The houses, their gardens, and the parks always looked neat, orderly and ordinary. It was as if the Second World War had omitted this location from its list of places to destroy. The image of Fuhlsbüttel as an oasis would have been complete except for the steady march of refugees on its streets. For the most part, the forsaken didn't stay long in Fuhlsbüttel; it was just a road that led them north or south towards food. Yet some broke ranks and put down roots at a sprawling squatters' camp 200 metres from my observation post.

Since 1943, the camp had been a familiar landmark to the residents of Fuhlsbüttel. It had been established after Hamburg was firebombed. The city's homeless were encouraged by municipal government functionaries to immigrate to the empty, long-fallow fields near the airport and set up shanties. As Hamburg became more desolate and uninhabitable, the tent city grew and became a more permanent settlement. From the wreckage of their former homes, the inhabitants constructed wood huts that were an imperfect incarnation of their past lives. Eventually, shops and little industries sprang up in the squatters' camp to serve the needs of its citizens and the townspeople of Fuhlsbüttel. When the war concluded, the camp expanded to accommodate new refugees from the eastern edges of Germania. 'Go to Fuhlsbüttel,' they were told, 'you will get better rations being shoulder to shoulder with the RAF.'

It was rumoured that within its canvas and scrap wood confines, some of the best tradesmen in northern Europe now resided. Friede told me: 'If you are brave, you should go into the camp because they have wonderful dressmakers and unique jewellery for sale, from cash-strapped Prussian Junkers.'

Her suggestion wasn't subtle, it wasn't nuanced; it was a reminder to me that she considered her eighteenth birthday an important milestone that should be celebrated with an appropriate gift. At the time, bargains were as common as pennies, but my salary was only £2.10 a week. The squatters' camp was my best option to locate an object I could afford for her birthday.

When my shift ended, I left the tower and slipped on a pair of aviator sunglasses. At the base of the observation tower, a group of clerks huddled together by the side of the telephone exchange entrance, smoking cigarettes. I knew them from my regular, weekday occupation.

'Fancy a beer, Harry?'

'No thanks, maybe later. I've got to get my girlfriend a present for her birthday.'

'Yer German bird?' one of them asked.

'Girlfriend,' I responded. '"Bird" is for pubs and bowling on a Tuesday night. She's my girl.'

'Sure she is,' the airman responded caustically. 'Those Fräuleins are all out for one thing, a good time, until the brass runs out. Then they'll bugger off to get a new mate to luv 'em.'

I ignored his comment. There was no time to waste because I had to go to the armoury before I left camp. RAF regulations required that all personnel carry a firearm while off the base. It was a precaution in case there were civil disturbances by disgruntled Germans.

The airman in charge of weapons opened the lock-up and handed me a weapon, along with a warning. 'Try not to shoot yourself with it. Last night two of our boys were wounded from glass shrapnel after they opened a clip into a lorry of empty bottles.'

'I'll keep that in mind.'

I don't know what I would have done if I had been faced with a situation requiring the use of my gun. I would have turned and fled or used the gun as a blunt instrument rather than discharge it. My only experience with a firearm was in England, during my numerous RAF training exercises. It only proved to me and my drill instructor that I was no rifleman. My targets, like the milk bottles at a carnival, were safe from harm with my wild aim.

I quickly left the armoury. My Sten gun was strung around my shoulder as if I were a gangster. At the entrance to the air base, the guard called out, 'Up to some of yer monkey business, Harry?'

'Not today, Tom, I'm just out for a parson's stroll.'

I moved along the perimeter of the airfield towards the haphazard city of the dispossessed. The wind picked up and scattered dead leaves, dirt, and an army of young boys hunting for cigarette ends around me.

'Zigaretten?'

'You're too young to be smoking,' I muttered and tossed them some loose sweets from my trouser pocket.

The young boys scattered like the blowing leaves and the dirt around us. In between the gusts of wind, I heard them gibber thanks and curse me in German. As the children moved away, the refugee camp quickly came into my full focus. It looked even more jumbled from the ground than from my lofty air traffic control tower. The encampment stretched from the end of one desolate field to the next. It was a community strung together with canvas and wood and fastened unhappily by the glue of desperation.

There wasn't an official entrance to the shanty town. There was no sign announcing 'You are now entering the refugee camp', there was no bridge to cross, and no toll to pay. I just walked between some huts and sauntered into the shambles.

Inside the camp it was as claustrophobic as an ancient slum. Everything was built tightly together, with one building using another structure as support. Rope, nails and luck seemed to be the only things holding the flimsy buildings upright. Most were ready to collapse into dust when the next strong storm burst into the camp.

It was an awful place, and within these thin walls made from bomb debris, people lived like the forsaken with little time for laughter or love. Coming from every tent or wood structure, I smelt the seeping stink of an over-ripe tip. Between the dense smell of decay, there was an odour of soups, heavy on cabbage being boiled to oblivion, that drifted through the air like a virus.

Around me, old women with brooms made from coarse tree branches swept the dirt and dust into organised piles. They looked me over strangely, as if I were a tourist from an ocean liner come to port for a one-day stopover.

At first the residents seemed distrustful towards me, until, like a pack of dogs, their noses sniffed and determined I was harmless. The first to approach was a shoemaker who jumped out from a tiny wooden stall. The skinny cobbler wore a leather apron and a patch over his right eye. A leather workman's cap rested on his head as if it had been placed there at his birth. 'Mein Herr!' he yelled out and introduced himself. 'Gut to meet.' The cobbler thrust out his hand to me, which was caked in dirt.

I refused to embrace it with a quick shake of my head. Nervously, he plunged it back to his side, where he began wiping it down across his apron.

'I have for you excellent shoes, best price, no shit, only excellent leather, Mein Herr. I give only the best for you, being such a fine officer.'

'I'm not an officer, mate,' I said, and tried to step around him and make my way down the lane.

'No, please, shoes are good,' he said, blocking my exit.

'Don't need shoes. The RAF provides me with proper boots.'

'Maybe you need a belt?'

I looked down at my frayed, ageing belt and agreed with him.

He pulled off his cap and scratched a bald head as if thinking how he might fleece me. He began to grin at me with a jack-o'-lantern mouth containing three black teeth. 'Forty cigarettes and I sell you one.'

'You're off your bicycle,' I replied. 'I must have made the wrong turn and ended up on the High Street in Manchester.'

'*Was?*' he asked.

'Never mind,' I replied.

'Twenty cigarettes,' he said with similar enthusiasm.

'Four cigarettes,' I responded with the voice of a seasoned barterer, which I wasn't.

Downcast, the shoemaker was about to return to his tiny stall when he cried out: 'For you, a friend, I can do it for five cigarettes.'

'Done,' I replied in a matter-of-fact tone.

'Tommy, give me the cigarettes now.'

'No, I think I will wait and see what you have to offer first.'

The shoemaker measured my waist with a greasy piece

of string and then returned to his cubby hole. In it were strands of leather with different dimensions and belt buckles. I wondered if his entire inventory was purloined from the morgue, but thought it best not to question the provenance of his goods. He fished out a belt for my approval, which had a giant metallic buckle.

'Too flashy,' I said.

The cobbler scrounged around for a while longer at the back of his stall. Triumphantly, he thrust a belt into the air as if he had pulled a trout from a river and called out, 'Is this besser?'

'That will do just fine,' I told him.

'Wunderbar, my good Sergeant Tommy,' he said, handing me the belt.

'Hey, Fritz, I'm not a sergeant. Look at the badge. I'm just a bloody wireless operator. I'm like the girl at the Altona hotel, I just transfer calls to the penthouse suite.'

'You should be a sergeant.'

'Sure,' I said, 'and you should have a proper shop but the world had other plans for us.'

There was some truth in the shoemaker's words. I could have been a sergeant, but declined the invitation because my mates said it was a bad idea. 'Like being bloody foreman down at mill,' said one. 'Once you start wearing stripes, you'll be having your pints alone.'

So in a foolish spirit of comradeship, I declined the promotion as I wished to remain with my fellow LACs. However, there was one in my group who was shrewder than me. He wisely calculated that the raise in pay and stature, and the grander possibilities, outweighed drinking alone and volunteered to wear the patch on his sleeve in my place.

'OK, Tommy. See, Mein Herr, I am the best. No disappointments with my work.'

I handed him the agreed five cigarettes, which he grabbed anxiously.

'You come back again, Tommy,' he said. 'I am good business.'

As I was about to move on, I asked him: 'Hey, Fritz, I'm looking for some nice jewellery, a brooch or a necklace.'

He thought for a while and said, 'Go up ten stalls. There is a widow, some officer's wife from Prussia. All fancy and fine; she has got things for sale. But don't let her cheat you; she is a crafty old crow.'

I walked away from his stall and moved further into the village of refugees. Children with dirty faces and torn clothing ran past me, reminding me of my own miserable youth. It was easy to find the Prussian widow's quarters because it was near a communal bog. She looked to be in her late fifties. Her hair was streaked with grey and she wore a smart dress and flat shoes, flaked with mud. At first, she didn't look at me when I spoke to her. Her wilted eyes were fixed on the children playing near the bog.

After a while, the widow responded. 'You want jewellery,' she said to me in perfect English. 'I have many interesting pieces that were given to me over the years. As you can see from my present circumstances, I have no use for ornaments. Please come inside,' she requested. The woman drew back a tent flap revealing a tiny living space with a camp bed and a broken dining chair.

Pointing to the chair, she said: 'Sit down if you like, but I am afraid it is not very comfortable.' By her bed, there was a picture of a man in a Wehrmacht uniform looking too proud for his own good. The woman noticed my gaze and said, 'My husband, in happier times. What are you looking for?'

I really didn't know. I had never bought jewellery for a woman before then, unless it was some cheap, shiny clasp from Woolworths.

'You are looking for something for your girlfriend?' inquired the widow.

'Yes, it is her birthday today.'

'What colour is her hair ... and her eyes?'

I told her. The woman smiled and said, 'She sounds very beautiful.' She added ruefully: 'It is a sad time to grow into German womanhood. I think I have something for you.'

The widow fetched a biscuit tin from underneath her bed. She lifted the lid and sorted through the stray bits and baubles from a bygone time. Eventually, she pulled out a sterling silver necklace pendant with a tiny sliver of fossilised amber mounted into the delicate metalwork. Its beauty was simple. It wasn't ostentatious, but quietly elegant and sensual. The widow saw my appreciation for the jewellery.

'It was my daughter's,' she said in an empty voice.

'How much is it?' I asked.

'A carton of cigarettes,' said the widow, as she handed me the jewellery so I could feel the workmanship. 'It's real silver,' she asserted.

I didn't haggle and handed over the required sum.

As I left, the widow said, 'I hope it brings more happy memories to your girlfriend than it has to me.'

CHAPTER 10

The birthday party

I stumbled through my love affair with Friede in igno-
rance and youthful lust. I had neither a map to chart my
affair nor a lexicon to define its development. In truth, I
didn't even have a compass to show me the true direction
where love might be found. My past was certainly not a reliable guide; it harboured only betrayal, hunger and familial
misdeeds. As for my previous love affairs, they were few,
brief, and about as satisfying as eating soggy chips in a
November rain. So, it was only natural for me to believe
that my developing attachment to Friede was beyond my
learning experiences.

Even a birthday party was an exotic occurrence for me.
Friede's eighteenth birthday was the first coming-of-age
celebration I had ever attended. For my own eighteenth
birthday I prepared for induction to the RAF, where I was
to be taught to kill or be killed by Germans. Now my only
apprehension about Germans was whether Friede's mother
was going to find me an acceptable match for her daughter.

Friede had described her mother from so many different angles, I began to think of her as a cubist canvas of vice
and virtue, coloured by sacrifice and sensuality. To Friede,
her mother was impossible, glamorous, selfish and loving.
In sentimental moments, Friede showed me pictures of her
mother and said, 'Wasn't she beautiful?' The studio portraits

revealed an attractive woman, but I also noticed steel in her beauty, flashing from her eyes.

On my way to the birthday party, I fretted that her mother was going to dismiss me as unworthy because I lacked their Continental outlook. I dreaded a cold rebuff similar to my treatment by Friede's foster mother, Frau Bornholt. She had accepted me as a sort of English delivery boy who was welcome to stand at the apartment entrance while she took my gifts from the RAF storehouse.

When I arrived, Friede was waiting for me at the front entrance to the apartment. She rushed over to greet me. I kissed her and whispered into her ear, 'Happy birthday.'

'Thank God you are here.'

'Why?'

'Mutti and Grandfather have been fighting for the last hour because the old man keeps stealing the cigarettes you gave me. The old Nazi cuckold says he has a right to everything because we are all horrible, immoral women. What a crazy man he is. I think Oma must have died to get away from him. Let me take those flowers from you. Mutti is dying to meet you and has been practising the English expressions I taught her. I am afraid she has not had much luck in pronouncing them correctly.'

I hope it's not 'bugger off', I thought.

Friede's mother stood at the top of the landing by her opened apartment door. Maria Edelmann emitted a rehearsed warmth and welcome for my arrival; whether it was sincere or false was anyone's guess. She took my hand, affectionately kissed me on both cheeks and spluttered out some fractured English – 'Velcom, you to mein Haus, gut'

– and escorted me into their fashionably furnished apartment. Bucolic paintings of carefree vagabonds and laughing children adorned her hallway walls. The apartment's hardwood floors were covered with a series of worn Caucasian tribal carpets. In the background, the other guests chattered and laughed in staccato German.

Since the dining room was now occupied by the homeless Gellersons, Maria Edelmann ushered me to the kitchen. Inside, the Gellersons and Gerda huddled around a small table whose top was cluttered with cut up smoked sausages, schnapps glasses, and a crystal ashtray. A fresh breeze blew in from open french doors leading onto a balcony. The kitchen overlooked a hilly field and, in the far distance, a railway spur.

'Sit, sit,' her mother instructed me in the voice of an accomplished hostess. For the moment, I felt well looked after, although it seemed Maria Edelmann was treating me more like livestock that must be cuddled before being sent to the butcher's block.

'Mutti, don't fret over him. He is not made of glass,' Friede said with some irritation.

'It's all right,' I said, trying to defuse the tension.

'How was your day?' she asked.

I was about to respond when her mother interrupted to thank me for the supplies I had sent to prepare the birthday meal.

'It was nothing,' I responded. 'Frau Edelmann, it is always a pleasure to help you and your daughter.'

'Please call me Maria,' she said, with the precision of a coquette.

'Mutti,' Friede chortled at her mother. 'What about the stew?'

Her mother apologised and went over to the wood stove, while the Gellersons and Gerda approvingly sniffed the aroma coming from the cooking pot.

Friede took my arm and said, 'Let's go onto the balcony and have a cigarette.'

Outside, Friede said with a laugh, 'I thought I'd never be rid of her.' She whispered, 'We have been fighting all day like the dog and the cat.'

'Over what?'

'The dinner, of course,' she said. 'My mother is such a perfectionist when it comes to making a meal. I think that is how she trapped Uncle Henry. Of course, while Mutti prepared dinner Opa was a giant bore. He complained that nobody cared and said terrible things to Mutti. My mother retaliated by telling him she'd turn him out on his ear if he didn't smarten up.' Friede paused and then asked: 'Do you have a cigarette? I am dying for one. My mother doesn't like me smoking. She says it is just too modern for her. I don't know why it bothers her so much, considering Uncle Henry's business was in tobacco. It certainly kept her in fantastic dresses for years.'

'Friedl,' her mother called out from the kitchen, 'I have ears, so mind what you say out there.' This made everyone else in the kitchen laugh.

Friede sighed over her mother's comments and then asked, 'What do you think about girls smoking?'

'I like it,' I said. 'It makes them look like movie stars.'

'Me too,' she said, blowing blue smoke over the balcony and across into the open field. At that moment, she looked both distant and alluring, like a movie star on a billboard poster. Friede was wearing a yellow summer dress that was too thin for the cool weather outside and she began to shiver.

I offered her my tunic, but she refused and explained: 'It's old, I know. I bought it a long time ago, in the war. I really need new clothes, but there is so much else we need before fashion. I'd better see what Mutti is doing. Don't go anywhere,' she said playfully and stubbed her cigarette out.

'Even if the balcony catches on fire, I will remain until your return,' I replied in a lustful and longing voice, and whistled as she turned around to leave.

Friede laughed: 'See, my legs are now almost as good as Greta Garbo's because the medicine you gave me really worked. Look how those horrible wounds have turned into just blemishes. It's a pity my legs were not like that in the summer.'

Friede left me alone for five minutes or so and then popped her head out from the small kitchen and asked, 'Harry, can you be a dear and fetch Opa? I imagine he is in the wood cellar, sulking. Give him one of your cigarettes; that will put him in the right mood.'

I said, 'What about opening the present I got you?'

'It will have to wait until after you get Opa. I want him to see me open my gifts. Maybe then, he will understand what my true friends think of me. It might even change his opinion about the Edelmann women,' she said with a laugh.

Maria Edelmann interrupted and said, 'Only when hell freezes over will that old man have a kind word for you or me.'

The warm smell of dinner trailed behind me as I left the apartment and walked down to the basement. In the cellar, there was a supply of neatly stacked wood, along with a collection of hutches holding rabbits for eating.

The cellar had a tiny window that allowed small particles of light to filter down into the dusky basement. I called out for Opa. There was no response. I crept around a wood pile, still calling his name. There was no reply except a thumping noise coming from the rabbit cages.

'Opa, I have an American cigarette for you,' I called, thinking that I could bribe him to come out from his hiding space. Again there was no answer. I thought we must have missed each other and the old bugger was already at the table slurping his soup.

'You are giving me a lot of trouble, Grandfather.' I put a cigarette to my lips and struck my Zippo lighter. Its flame illuminated a silhouette that was obscured by some boxes over to the right of me. I drew closer to investigate and soon realised the shadow was Opa and he was dead. The old man had committed suicide. His body was hanging from an old rope wrapped around a wooden beam running across the ceiling. A stain ran down his trouser legs. He had pissed himself when he had kicked the box over and begun to die from strangulation.

His lifeless body reminded me of the executed deserters I had seen while we drove into Germany just before the end of the war. He must have killed himself right after he stormed out of his stepdaughter's apartment. 'Well,' I said to the corpse, 'that will show them, hey, Opa.'

I righted the box and stood upon it to cut him down with my pocket knife, which was normally used to quarter apples. Now it sliced through the strands of rope inches above his skinny blue neck. When I was half-way through cutting the noose, the weight of his body snapped the last strands from the beam. The old man's corpse crashed to the dirt floor like a bushel of vegetables.

'Crikey,' I said in apology for Opa's undignified drop to earth. I pulled his crumpled body as straight as possible and regretted there was no blanket or tarpaulin handy to cover him.

Nothing that made him human remained. Everything was gone, even the hectoring; the jaded and jilted moaning had vanished from his old face. He just looked dead. His eyes were vacant and stared towards nothingness. I closed them shut and folded his hands over his chest. I stood beside his body and told him, 'Well, you were a right bastard, but now you can harm no one. So, wherever you are going, have a safe journey.'

When I got back to the apartment, everyone was seated around the kitchen table. They were waiting for me to return with Opa to begin the birthday dinner. Drinking from their wine glasses, they conversed in a lively and care-free fashion.

'What took you so long?' Friede asked. 'Where is Opa?'

Everyone's eyes were on me and I stammered for a bit. Finally, I blurted out, 'I'm sorry, Opa is dead.'

Friede asked in disbelief: 'Dead?'

Her mother took a sip of wine and laconically remarked: 'Tot.'

Her tone suggested to me that Maria didn't question his lack of existence, but wondered why it took so long. Everyone else was silent and embarrassed and looked as if a fart had been ejected into the atmosphere. I placed an opened cigarette pack on the table and watched hand after hand reach for the Player's.

Friede's mother spoke in a restrained tone. 'So the old so-and-so finally topped himself. Well, well, you would think it was my birthday. This is the first time that man has given me anything to be thankful for. Quite a gift he left us, hey, Friede.'

I was confused and somewhat offended by their reaction to the old man's departure.

'Gift?' I asked.

'Yes, he finally showed some good sense,' she said, toying with her glass of wine. 'It would have been rude and selfish of him to eat first and then kill himself. At the moment, death is more abundant than food in Hamburg. Still, he could have shown me the kindness of doing himself in at my sister's house. She at least was his natural daughter, while I was just the bastard child.'

'Mutti!' Friede screamed.

'Hush, Friede. Well, I suppose it is bad manners to speak ill of the dead.' Maria Edelmann sighed quietly and took a sip from her wine.

'Perhaps,' Friede suggested, 'Harry could go to the police and tell them about Opa. If he reports it, there will be no scandal because he is a Tommy.'

'Yes, of course,' I said. 'I will fetch a policeman. I won't be long.'

'I will keep your dinner warm,' Friede said, but as I left the apartment, I heard her mother doling out the stew by the spoonful to the other guests.

The police station was a quick stroll down the road. When I arrived, a duty sergeant in his twenties was sitting behind a desk, typing with one finger. In his immaculate police uniform, the copper looked as Prussian as Bismarck. After several seconds, the policeman noticed me. Even though he outranked me, the German stood to attention and saluted. I returned the salute and explained Opa's death. The policeman took out a notebook and asked for my name and the address where the incident occurred.

'You don't happen to have a spare cigarette on you?' he asked. I handed him a near-empty pack. 'Keep it, I have plenty more.'

'I don't see this as a problem,' said the policeman. 'It sounds like a pure and simple suicide.'

'Good,' I replied, 'the family has gone through enough as it is.'

'Yes,' he remarked, uninterested. 'Suicide is not an uncommon occurrence in Germany today. A lot of old people do away with themselves because they are a burden and they can't live with the defeat of Germany. Go back to your dinner. I will send a constable to the apartment to confirm the death. It is just a formality. I will telephone the morgue to expect the body. As a small piece of advice, it will probably be easier if you arrange for a truck to collect the suicide victim. There is no telling when

I could get a vehicle to gather the body. It might be quite some time.'

'How long is this going to take?'

'It could be a couple of days before I could get someone to fetch the body and by then the neighbours will complain of the stench coming from a decomposing body.'

The policeman let me use his telephone and I called the motor pool at the airfield. I arranged for a truck to take the body to the morgue. It cost me a week's wages, but it ended any threat of scandal or inconvenience over the hanging to either Friede or her mother.

When I returned to the apartment, the Gellersons had already decamped to their room. Friede and her mother were in an argument over the corpse in the basement, while Gerda cleaned up the dishes. I explained what I had done and Friede jumped from the table and hugged me affectionately.

'I don't know what we would have done without you,' she told me.

Maria remained seated, sipping her wine, as she complained: 'Even those who I disliked have deserted me. I have no one left to help me.'

'Oh Mutti,' Friede groaned. 'Stop your melodramatics.'

'What is she on about?' I asked.

'Nothing,' Friede said. 'It is the German affliction, Sturm und Drang.'

'Nothing,' Maria said. 'I have no one to rely upon since your Uncle Henry died.'

'Mutti, stop calling him Uncle Henry; he was your boyfriend. I am not a little girl any more. I know all about Henry. You were his kept woman.'

'Don't talk that way to me, child, not tonight, not ever. Maybe you will understand me better when you are grown up and not such a foolish teenager.'

I heard the RAF truck pull up outside. I asked Friede and her mother if they would like to go down to the morgue and say goodbye to the old man.

'No, I see no purpose in that,' said Maria. 'But I am now going downstairs to check his pockets. If he left any pfennigs, they are ours, not some orderly's.'

She thanked me for coming over for dinner and disappeared from the room. Friede looked at me apologetically. 'Now do you see why I don't want any drama in our relationship? I promise next time we will have a proper meal, but I think you should go now.'

'What about opening my gift?' I asked.

She kissed me on the lips and said afterwards, 'I am sorry, Harry. With all these theatrics going on, I don't feel like opening any presents. I promise I will open it soon with you.'

When I walked out of the door, she called out to me. 'Harry, I can't thank you enough for your help. I think maybe you are the one person who may come to understand me.'

Outside, the RAF driver had Opa's body draped over his shoulder like it was an overcoat.

'Do you need a hand?' I inquired.

'Nah, this bloke is as light as a baby,' he said, dropping him into the back of the truck like broken goods going off to the tip.

Maria Edelmann came outside and kissed me farewell.

She acted as if suicide and body disposal was a normal occurrence at a German birthday party.

When I got into the truck, the driver looked at me and said, 'Sometimes, it's probably best to stay at the NAAFI with feet on stool, near the fire.'

The truck started up with a bang and we pulled out towards the morgue, several blocks distant. When we drove away, I looked in the side-view mirror and caught sight of Friede standing with her mother and Gerda. They waved goodbye to me and good riddance to Opa, who was rolling around in the back of the lorry like an unsecured empty drum.

CHAPTER 11

Advent for the desolate

Hamburg's Indian summer struggled against November like a sputtering flame from a votive candle in a desolate church. Cold temperatures from the Scandinavian peninsula stomped into town and extinguished any optimism that the ice and sleet season would give us a miss at the end of 1945. Most days, the horizon was charcoal grey as the distant sun hid behind low clouds. In winter's chilly four o'clock light, the city's bombed out sections looked even more forsaken than during spring and summer. In the eleventh month, a frost covered the destroyed city like a cocoon.

When St Andrew's Day arrived, snowstorms raged up and down the northern tip of Germany. The brick Omas came out and swept the streets clean of snow with the same industriousness they used in June to clear the streets of war debris. As the mercury dropped, it became more difficult to provide supplies for malnourished Germans because roadways across Europe were closed due to the ferocious weather. The old, the sick, the young and the dispossessed died from exposure and incremental starvation. Decimation wasn't an official policy for Germany's collective sins; it was the product of inept bureaucratic planning. The government failed to make accurate projections. Their ledger books didn't have sufficient columns to calculate the effect of mass refugee migration to the western zones, nor could slide rules estimate starvation rates produced by the total collapse of agriculture and industrial output.

Yet as Germany slipped into hypothermia, famine and death, I was warm and well fed within our air base enclosure. Outside the fence, chaos and bedlam reigned supreme, but inside everything was routine and orderly. Every few days a plane arrived with fresh supplies and departed with demobbed men who had worn the King's uniform for long enough and were now allowed to return to Civvy Street. I was beginning to feel like the odd man out, as no one was left from my square-bashing days at Padgate at the war's beginning. Pretty well everyone I knew was gone. Even the men from my training days at St Athan and my pissed-up antics at Chigwell had packed up and buggered off home.

I was now surrounded by National Service virgins. They were five years my junior and when the sergeant major counted them in the mornings for King and country, these lads shouted out too eagerly their attendance and readiness for the RAF. I didn't share their neophyte enthusiasm. I acknowledged my presence with the familiarity of a cat being called to tea. An NCO once cried back, 'Almost time for your gold watch and farewell party, LAC Smith.'

At 22, I was an antique in the ranks of the stripeless RAF men of Fuhlsbüttel. Only two blokes remained from my first days in Germany: Sid Ward and Dave Needles. We chummed around and got drunk on the nights I wasn't busy with Friede. Sid stayed on in Germany because there wasn't much prospect for him back in the Midlands. 'When I go back,' he said, 'it is either as a man down the pit or as a pony down the pit. Not much difference, except the pony gets straw for his bed.' As for Dave, he stayed on for the adventure, but said he'd be heading home some time sooner rather than later because he missed his family in Nottingham.

I smiled and said, 'Sure, I know what you mean,' even though I couldn't comprehend Dave's hunger to return to his family. I couldn't get far enough away from mine or their grubby lives in Halifax. It didn't matter how much I wanted to renounce my kin, they weren't going to renounce me or my responsibilities to them. I received my mother's annual plaintive Yuletide letter, which as always was as succinct as cuneiform.

'Help out your poor old Mam. We're tight from all the rationing. Yer brothers need feeding and I am not getting any younger and my man Bill isn't pulling the wages he did before the war. Remember, son, it is soon Christmas time and we must all look out for t'other.'

I hastily sent my mother a letter which read: 'Mam: enclosed is £10; it should help you through Christmas. What I see in Germany today makes me weep and remember our own days ruined by starvation. I am sure the pounds I've sent will keep your chin up, at least until New Year's Day. Your loving son, Harry.'

My six-month extension with the RAF was almost up. It didn't take the toss of a coin for me to know that I wanted to remain in Germany: Friede was here and unhappy memories of England were across the sea. There was no opposition from the RAF to my request and I was granted an extension of service. They were happy to oblige, as I was a trusted and experienced old man on base who could be relied upon to do my duties at both air traffic control and switchboard operations. At least the Air Ministry believed it had got its money's-worth by training me and not killing me during the conflict.

During my almost five years in the RAF, I developed a good rapport with my superiors. In Fuhlsbüttel, the NCOs and officers knew me to be a capable individual not prone to tattle after school. I was granted extraordinary privileges because of my reputation for competence and discretion.

I even requested a change in my sleeping quarters.

'You what?' asked a sergeant. 'You want to move from barracks to your own room? It's a bit early in the morning to be asking me for a 'ouse. Why don't you try for something smaller first, like a bleeding blanket or an extra towel?'

'I'm not asking for a 'ouse, Sergeant. It's nothing that grand. It's no bigger than a cubby hole; it's just an unused room on base that would do nicely for my sleeping quarters.'

'Where is this hidey-hole?' he asked suspiciously.

'It's on the second floor in the air traffic control tower. If I was allowed to kip there, I'd never be late for a shift again,' I responded encouragingly.

The NCO looked around as if he had been asked to sneak a woman onto our military enclosure. He contemplated my suggestion and after a while he shrugged his shoulders. 'Smith, as long as you don't turn it into a pub, pawn shop, or apothecary, it's all right with me. I'll square it with the muckedy mucks and then it's yours. Mind you, if you fuck this up, Smith, your next 'ouse will be the dog 'ouse.'

My new quarters were the best digs I'd ever lived in, aside from my brief stay in a Dutch villa on our way to Hamburg. To make my lodgings complete, I commandeered a giant double bed from storage, which had once given gentle sleep to a Luftwaffe officer. Now, it cradled me like a baby. It was far better than the straw-filled mattresses I normally slept on. I was even able to trade some coffee to a dodgy motor-pool mechanic and get a portable wireless radio. Tuned to Armed Forces Radio, it entertained me between my work shifts, with crooners singing about unhappy love affairs or comedians gently pulling the leg of military life.

My quarters even had a writing desk where I arranged my slim collection of books: Wordsworth's sonnets, Saint-Exupéry, and some novels by Dickens.

The desk stood at the back of the room beneath a large window that opened up onto an expansive view of the neighbourhood. When I was off duty, I'd smoke cigarettes while perched up on its cold ledge. In between blowing smoke rings, I tried to make out which snow-covered rooftop was Friede's apartment, while dreaming of our next encounter.

Having my own quarters in the communications tower was a definite advantage to my love affair with Friede. The building worked on a 24-hour cycle, meaning no one took any notice of my presence or absence from the building. Living there allowed me to ignore curfew because no one was checking up on me. It was easy for me to sneak out of the camp; I just hopped over the barbed wire enclosure behind the tower. It was my preferred exit because the guards at the main gate had begun to conduct random searches for stolen RAF food supplies and medicine. The looting of RAF stores was becoming too common and too enormous for the brass to ignore. So the officers tried to stop a flood of racketeering by dropping a sandbag against a river. It might have blocked the small-time entrepreneur, but the bigger operators were never searched because they never walked out of camp, they drove.

My capacity to disappear over the wire increased as we came closer to the holiday season. I preferred to spend my time in Friede's company rather than the enforced jovialness produced at the camp canteen. During that December, there was little cheer on the streets of Hamburg. The Germans were sombre and subdued, burying their feelings about Christmas under the heavy coats they wore while trading away their history on the black markets. Their grim looks were understandable because many were too preoccupied mourning their war dead to follow the rituals of celebrations. Even in Friede's apartment, the inhabitants were sullen. They all wore an aggrieved look as they ground their teeth in angst over the question: what happens next?

Maria Edelmann and the elderly Gellersons were exceptionally gloomy because they remembered the anarchy that fell upon Hamburg after the Great War.

'Back then, it was civil war,' said Herr Gellerson, while his wife nodded in agreement.

Maria Edelmann retorted: 'If the Tommies don't sort out the food crisis, it will be war again. The Germans will only take so much and rise up against them.'

'Hush, Mutti,' Friede, said. 'Don't talk your nonsense in front of Harry.'

After six months of occupation, life was getting worse not better for them. Their only supply of fresh food above their calorie allotment came from me. Maria Edelmann was no romantic and understood that my love for her daughter was a precarious rope to hang on to for salvation. Their pessimism lingered around the apartment like incense. Only a week away from Christmas and there was no tree, no candles, nor any sign of the approaching holiday in their lodgings.

One evening, before I left Friede to sneak back into camp, I asked in a rather cold-hearted fashion whether Germans celebrated Christmas. Friede responded sarcastically: 'We did until the British reduced our fat and milk rations and said Happy Christmas.'

It was a cold goodnight kiss for me. Before I could offer an apology, she slammed the door shut and I left with my tail between my legs.

I walked back to camp through dark and quiet streets, while overhead a clear sky was punctured by distant cold stars. I wasn't a sentimentalist and my memories of Christmas were as pleasant as an abscessed tooth. As a lad, they were bleak and unhappy occasions spent with my sister at a Catholic church charity. The almshouse was short on toys but long on sermons about the grace of poverty. The Christmases of my past taught me that it's best to expect little from others, and that too much gin produced a sad cheer on my mother, who had run out of hope.

I don't know what made me double back that night to Friede's apartment, except maybe guilt over my cynicism. When I reached the building, I sneaked into the basement, where I found an axe they used to cut firewood. I grabbed it and walked towards the field opposite the back of their dwelling. The snow was fresh and it felt like walking into the shallow edges of a lake. In the middle of the pasture, just below the hill leading to the railway spur, I found some blue spruces that were around two metres in height. I took the axe to one of them and chopped through the base of the tree. I dragged it back through the snow to Friede's mother's place.

When I placed it to the side of Friede's apartment door, the tree smelt of resin and the cold winter's night. I banged loudly and ran back out into the street. As I walked down Langenhorner Chaussee, I heard the main apartment door swing open. Friede called out: 'Danke schön, Mein Harry!'

I turned around and saw her standing in her nightgown. She waved to me and I returned her gesture with a silent bow.

In the last mail before Christmas, parcels and letters arrived from my mother and my sister. I took the packages to my room and put them on my desk. I retrieved a bottle of brandy from my writing desk and poured a shot of 'eau de vie' into a tin mug. I opened my sister's parcel first. There wasn't much to it: a photo of her with her son, a note about people I didn't know, from a world I was trying to forget. She had enclosed a scarf and a postscript that read: 'To keep yourself warm and snug, think of it like my hugs, when we were wee and you were as frozen as an icicle because there was no coal in the grate.' She thanked me for my gift of money; she said it would buy a nice pair of shoes for her boy Derek. She ended the missive with: 'I'd luv to see ya home, but I think you haven't yet found a place for your heart to kip.'

In my mother's small parcel were Christmas greetings from her, her lover Bill the cowman, and my two half-brothers. She thanked me for the money I'd sent and also enclosed a wristwatch. Its value was ten shillings or less. The watch was light and flimsy to my touch. I wasn't offended by the cheapness of the timepiece; it was the paucity of time my mother had employed to consider my gift. My Mam probably bought it in a rush, while storming past a second-rate shop window on her way to or from a pub. I handled the watch with a mixture of curiosity and disdain; I wondered about her commitment to me. Was she at least as loyal as a mother bird to its young? 'Now you can fly, bugger off, because Mam's got another kid on her tit.'

My musings were interrupted by a knock at the door. I hid the watch underneath some papers, but left my sister's scarf exposed. It was Sid.

'Do you fancy going out for a beer?'

I said sure.

'What are you doing for Christmas Eve?' Sid asked.

'I'm with Friede and her family.'

'Lucky bugger, you should hook me up with Gerda, your girl's best friend, so I can get some kisses for New Year.'

'I'll see what I can do. Give me a minute,' I said, 'and I'll meet you downstairs.'

Sid left and closed the door behind him. I picked up the watch and looked at its cheap face. I wondered about the past and the time spent with my mother during our days of starvation. That night, I couldn't decide whether she was the sin, the sinner, or the one sinned upon, or whether it even mattered. I buried my mother's present deep in the drawer of my desk; for all I cared, it could lie there until time stopped. I picked up my sister's scarf and wrapped it around my neck, turned out the lights, left my room, and went outside to meet up with Sid.

CHAPTER 12

Stille Nacht

It snowed on Christmas Eve. It fell like icing sugar and dusted the city as if it were a stale and crumbling Christmas cake. The peddlers, black marketeers and cigarette hustlers scrambled to finish their commerce before the church bells pealed to celebrate the birth of Christ. Along the St Pauli district, steam-powered trucks delivered beer and wine to the whorehouses, which expected exceptional business from nostalgic servicemen. Across the Reeperbahn the lights burned bright, while in the refugee camps the homeless huddled down against the cold, warming themselves with watery soup and kind words provided by visiting Lutheran priests.

The airport was somnolent; the servicemen charged with keeping it operational were as sluggish as a cat curled up on a pillow before a fire. Outside the communications tower, LACs took long cigarette breaks, draped in their greatcoats. In between puffs and guffaws, they swapped lewd jokes or tales about their sexual exploits with German women.

The air traffic control nest was unmanned for the next few days. The radio transmitters hummed emotionlessly because the ether above was empty and the clouds ripe for snow. Nothing was expected to arrive or depart until Boxing Day. On the ground, the roadways around the airport were quiet because the fleet of RAF vehicles was stabled at the motor pool for the duration of the holiday. Everywhere it was still, except on the runway where a platoon of new recruits cleared snow from the landing area.

At the telephone exchange, the switchboard was staffed by a bored skeleton crew who waited for their shift to end. The normal frenetic noise and activity from hundreds of calls being patched and dispatched through the camp to the military world in Germany and Britain was hushed as there were few people left to either place or receive a call. Some communications operators hovered around mute teletype machines, which awoke every hour and furiously printed out wind speed, temperature and ceiling levels – 'For bloody Saint Nick,' someone remarked.

This was a unique Christmas because for the first time since 1938, the entire world was at peace. So anyone who was able took leave, and abandoned our aerodrome for a ten-day furlough. For those of us who remained, a Christmas committee was formed to organise festivities. The Yule spirit around camp mirrored that of terraced-house Britain. It was constructed out of cut-price lager and crêpe paper decorations with the unspoken motto: 'Cheap but cheerful cheer in Fuhlsbüttel.' In the mess hall, a giant Christmas tree was erected dangerously close to a wood stove by the Xmas team. They had festooned it with glittering ornaments and placed faux presents underneath its boughs. Sleighs and Father Christmas figures cut from heavy paper were pinned to the walls as festive decorations. Mistletoe dangled from light fixtures and gave our dining hall the appearance of a holiday party at a carpet mill in Halifax.

On the morning before Christmas, I negotiated with the head cook for extra rations for Friede and her family to allow them a holiday meal. The cook was an obliging Londoner whose mastery of the culinary arts began and ended with the breakfast fry-up. Never one to say no to sweetening his own pot, the cook amicably took my bribe of tailored shirts in exchange for food. He let me fill my kit bag to bursting with tinned meat, savouries and sweets.

'Give the Hun a bit of a treat tonight,' he said. 'Take the pork pie along with a bit of plum pudding.'

'What about some cheeses?'

'Sure, I've got plenty, could be a bleeding monger at the market with all the Gouda and Edam,' the cook said. 'No cheddar though; it's for the toffs with shiny clogs.'

From a cheese wheel, he cut a week's portion of Gouda and wrapped it in wax paper for me.

'Hold on a moment,' he said, walking to a cabinet that contained wine, spirits and beer. The cook removed some champagne and bottled ale for my parcel. He cautioned: 'Mind you don't get caught with this. Give my best to the missus. Pity I can't give you a trifle, but it would spoil on the way.' As I departed, he called out, 'Happy Christmas. Remember, mum's the word.'

'Are we still on for next week?' I asked.

'If you bring shirts as soft as this one, I am always open for business to you,' he said, stroking my bribe as if it were a dog. 'Now, off with ya. Can't you see I have lunch to prepare for you useless and thankless lot?'

'Don't burn the water and have a Happy Christmas,' I replied and left the cookhouse.

It was late in the afternoon before I had a drink with Sid, Dave and some other mates at the canteen. We played several games of skittles where I displayed my poor gamesmanship. I lost a few shillings, but redeemed myself with a good showing in darts. Through each drag on my cigarette, I nervously wondered when it was expedient to sneak out of camp to go to Friede's with my bag of food and Christmas gifts.

The minute hand on the wall clock walked slowly through another hour of conversation about football clubs and Christmases back in Britain: 'They were magic.'

So everyone agreed – including me – that the holidays at home were magic, and we drank more beer to celebrate those 'bloody magic days of youth'. To myself, I thought Christmas was more witchcraft than magical in the 'dirty thirties', but I wasn't going to spoil this celebration by denying their belief in happy childhood memories. I just wanted to depart and have a 'bloody magic moment' on Christmas Eve 1945. The minute hand moved reluctantly forward like a prisoner on his way to the gallows. It was time to go and I swallowed down my beer in one mouthful.

I patted Sid on the back and said, 'Don't wait up for me.'

'Tara,' he responded, with a half pint of bitter in his glass and foam racing around his lips.

'Are you going over the top or charging through the gate tonight?'

'Straight ahead – the bloke on duty will look the other way with a pack of Christmas fags.'

On my way to Friede's, the streets were cold, desolate and empty of pedestrians. Anyone with a place to stay was already safely tucked warmly inside. When I arrived at the steps of the apartment, it was just after eight. I hesitated at the front door and nervously adjusted my hair. From inside I heard Christmas carols float out from the wireless. Self-conscious and unskilled at family situations, I hoped I wasn't going to make an ass of myself or reveal my poor upbringing. Just as I was about to ring the bell, Friede swung the door open. She looked confident, happy, and flushed from drink. In the background, I heard her mother talking to Frau Gellerson.

'Hello, Happy Christmas,' I said in a voice that sounded as if I was unsure of the correct greeting.

'Merry Christmas, Harry, come in. You must be cold. Let me take your coat.' Friede slipped it off my shoulders and placed it onto the standing rack. After I slid off my boots, she took my hand and said, 'Let's go and say hi to everyone.'

'In a moment,' I said. 'I want to stay here for a while longer and have you all to myself. You look so wonderful.' She blushed at the compliment and her eyes sparkled with the sensuality of youth.

Friede was wearing a delicate black wool jumper with a slender skirt and dark nylon stockings that ran seductively up her legs. Around her delicate long neck dangled the necklace I had bought for her birthday. Her lips were coloured with a faint rouge, while her raven hair was combed back and had a light, perfumed scent of spring flowers.

'You look so beautiful,' I stammered.

Friede blushed and whispered, 'I did this for you.'

I was about to respond when her mother shouted out:

'For heaven's sake, bring him inside, he is not a tradesman come to fix the plumbing.'

Friede ushered me into the kitchen, where her mother was preparing a fish soup for the evening meal. The Christmas tree stood at the right-hand side of the entrance. On its branches, lit candles burned from their holders and cast warm shadows across the room.

'Harry,' Maria Edelmann said with a note of accomplishment in her voice, 'I actually found carp in a market today.'

'Mutti, you didn't find the whole fish, just the heads,' Friede interjected.

'It was still a miracle, considering that the British with their private restaurants and clubs are gobbling up all the best Christmas foods.' She wiped her hands on an apron that protected a very becoming evening dress. Maria walked over to me and greeted me with a kiss and said, 'Instead of carp for dinner, we will have bouillabaisse, which will be just fine.'

'I've brought some things that should help with the festivities.' I opened up my satchel and produced the wine, the meat pies, the cheeses and cakes. The women cooed in appreciation at the additions while Herr Gellerson looked at the wine and approved the vintage.

'Harry, choose a wine quickly,' Friede exclaimed, 'because I am slowly dying from this homemade schnapps.'

Herr Gellerson interjected, 'I could sell it on the black market as petrol and we would all be rich.'

I easily opened the cork to the French sparkling wine, but I recklessly over-filled our glasses and spilled much of it onto the table. After a hasty toast, the Gellersons retreated to their room and Friede's mother resumed dinner preparations. I disappeared with Friede into her tiny sleeping alcove where we talked and kissed.

'I should give you your present now,' I said, excited like a schoolboy looking for approval.

'No,' she said putting her finger to my lips. 'We will eat first. Just before midnight, we open up our gifts. It is custom. It is silly that you do not know this. What on Earth did you do in England for Christmas?'

I smiled and said, 'Things are different there. We opened presents in the morning.' To myself I thought, if you were lucky to get one.

Friede changed the subject and started to smoke a cigarette.

'There is a lot of gossip going around these days about Germans being forced into work details around the city.'

'This is news to me,' I replied.

'I think it is true,' she said with a note of seriousness in her voice. 'I have heard the British and the new German civilian authorities are going to send German women to work.'

'Work where?'

'In any factories that are still functional. There is also talk of German entrepreneurs returning from abroad. They made deals with the British to build their manufacturing empires on cheap labour as punishment to the Germans who stayed with Hitler. Like we had a choice,' Friede added sarcastically.

'What type of deal?'

'Don't be a dummkopf, the oldest agreement in the

world: I scratch your back, you scratch mine. It is bribes, liebchen, old-fashioned cash bribes.'

'But why are they going to force the women to work in these places?'

'There is no one left in Germany but women and babies. All of our German men are either dead or in concentration camps in Russia. Anyway, if this happens, we will be treated like the foreign workers were under the Nazis. I don't think I could survive under those conditions.'

'I've never heard anything about this,' I said, 'but I am sure it will have nothing to do with you.'

'I hope not,' she said, unconvinced. She curled up a leg behind her and became child-like. 'I want this holiday, this New Year to be special. During the war, Christmas was very sad with so many causalities at the front and so much destruction around at home. I never felt safe and it never felt particularly joyful.'

'I will try to make this Christmas a happy time for us,' I said, convinced I could alter history.

Friede didn't sound persuaded, and asked: 'What is going to become of us next year? We get poorer by the day. Mutti is getting older. Look, even her hair has turned grey because she is all alone with no one to look after her. I don't think she will find another man like Henry to take care of her and protect her at her age.'

'What about your real father?' I asked.

Friede sighed. 'Poor Fritz, he never got to know me. I wonder what he would have thought about me. You know, through my childhood, he did write to me and sometimes he sent me birthday cards. The last letter I got from him was in January. He was working in Berlin at an army truck factory. He said he was an engine fitter.'

'What else did he say?' I asked.

'Oh, you know, the same old Fritz. "Let's get to know each other better, you are my only daughter." I wrote him back to say that after ignoring his only daughter for all of those years, I was doing just fine without him.'

'Did he write back?'

'No, he was probably killed defending Berlin from the Russians like most of the other old men and boys who were press-ganged into the Volkssturm. Anyway, I haven't heard anything from him since his last letter to me. But who knows with Fritz, maybe he will show up one day with a fantastic story to tell.'

'I'm sorry about your father,' I said.

'It doesn't matter, I never knew him. Papa was the only man who was like a real father to me. Poor Papa, he is out of work and too old to help me with anything. So you see, Harry, I have no one to protect me. I am just a German girl among millions with no money or influence.' She sighed and continued, 'I will never be able to finish my education and I am useless at anything practical. The world has enough dreamers. So what am I going to do?'

'Don't worry,' I said. 'I will always help and things do get better.'

'How?' she asked caustically. 'Germans and Tommies aren't supposed to fraternise. Sure, you can have a German girlfriend, but a German wife is verboten by Britain. They don't want us to have a future together. So don't make promises you can't keep, Harry.'

I was about to dispute her claim, but decided it was pointless to get into an argument over official policy. She was correct; the authorities in charge didn't want us to develop deep or lasting relations with Germans. The unwritten code promoted by the British military government was: trade with them, steal from them, fuck them, but for God's sake don't fall in love with them. The last thing England needed was a bunch of half-breeds in lederhosen sapping reserves off council boards.

When dinner was called, the Gellersons brought out a gramophone and set it up in the kitchen. Over dinner, we listened to ancient pre-war 78rpm discs of German carols or nostalgic songs about Hamburg sung by soloists. During the meal, there was an element of make-believe to our conversation and in the expression and gestures of the diners. Between mouthfuls of soup and warm bread, my hosts remembered and relived old Christmases when there was no war and their life was not dictated by occupation. Maria Edelmann, the Gellersons and Friede laughed at old worn jokes. They spoke about people now missing from their lives but who at one time had passed over their hearts and left a shadow.

Friede turned to me and smiled as if to say, 'All these old people and their memories; I will make a thousand better ones.' Watching them, I understood that I was an outsider looking into their world. It was a universe of memories from a collapsed galaxy. It was odd that even though their lives had been so horribly altered by the war and their present filled with hunger and pessimism, they were still thankful for being alive.

Their stories about better days grew as thin as the candles burning on the tree and a melancholy fell across the room as the evening dwindled down towards midnight. Friede and her mother looked as soft and sad as English rain. Their hearts ached for a finished era, dead family, friends and lovers.

'Harry, fill up everyone's wine glass,' Friede instructed and stood to toast Christmas Eve. 'To life, to being alive, and to all of us being fed, healthy, and happy,' she proclaimed.

Everyone clapped and drank. I noticed Maria Edelmann drained the entire contents of her glass and quickly refilled it with a trembling hand.

Maria then asked me, 'So does your own mother make such a feast on Christmas Eve?'

I lied and said, 'On Christmas Day, my Mam puts out a roast goose with all the trimmings,' whereupon everyone enviously applauded my fictitious family festivities.

'Look at the time,' Herr Gellerson said, consulting his pocket watch. 'It is almost midnight; we should exchange gifts.'

Another bottle of wine was opened while Friede handed out presents from under the tree. From Maria Edelmann I received a small book of Schiller's poetry and the Gellersons presented me with a pair of socks. When Friede opened up my gift, her eyes became as effervescent as champagne bubbles.

'What is it?' her mother asked.

'It is so wonderful,' Friede said. 'Everyone come here and have a look at it.'

She held up an exquisite silver bracelet on which each link in the chain was a tiny silver elephant. Friede clapped her hands and said, 'This is fantastic,' as she placed it on her wrist for everyone to admire. Friede then handed me an envelope and said nervously, 'I hope this is all right, I hope you understand.'

Inside the envelope was a large photo of Friede. The portrait showed her wearing the necklace I had bought for her birthday. My hands shook as I absorbed the photo and everyone around me faded away from consciousness.

Friede smiled invitingly from the photo and I swam in the depth of her eyes. They shone out from the picture and radiated a singular love for me. On the back of the photograph was inscribed: 'Für Meine Harry, Ich Liebe Dich.'

'Do you like it?' she asked apprehensively.

I was silent and she repeated the question and woke me from my dreams. 'Yes,' I responded quietly.

'It was very difficult for me to find a photographer, let alone someone with developing fluid and paper to make the portrait. There is literally nothing left in Hamburg to make photos.'

I leaned over to kiss her and said thank you a thousand times. I was overwhelmed and excused myself and went to get some air on the balcony. In the cold quarter-to-midnight air, I lit a cigarette and felt the wind dry my face stained with tears.

Friede came out onto the balcony and asked if I was OK. 'Yes,' I replied. 'Your present was beautiful,' I told her in a breaking voice.

'What is it, then? Why are you so sad?' she said.

'Not sad, it's just, before this, no one ever gave me a gift like yours. It's hard to explain but I don't think anyone has ever said they love me like you did in the photo.'

'No one?' she asked in disbelief.

'Not a one,' I said. 'Neither my father nor mother ever really said they loved me. There was only my sister Mary who said she loved me before you. She'd say it when we went to bed as children, hungry and dirty from scrounging coal to try to keep our house warm.'

Friede, with wide open and caring eyes, kissed my hand and said, 'Well, I love you. Our past lives are history. Let's just try to love each other and hope it will survive the winter and the occupation.'

Maria Edelmann and the Gellersons came out onto the balcony. They held lit candles to confront winter's darkness. With one arm around Friede and my other hand holding on to a burning taper, I heard the bells across the city strike midnight. As the bells rang, people from neighbouring apartments stepped onto their balconies, also holding lit candles. Eventually, the clamour from the bells drifted away and all that remained was an expectant emptiness in the air. A male voice stirred from four apartments away. He began in a low, strong tone, singing the words to 'Silent Night'. His voice was joined by other singers until the melody reached our balcony; we also sang Brahms' lullaby to mankind. The tune travelled deep into the blackened city and dissipated into the Elbe River, where it drifted out to the cold, dark Baltic Sea.

CHAPTER 13

Winter 1946

Around Epiphany, the colour of the sky over Hamburg changed from a watery, drab white to the grey pallor of death. The heavens dropped low over the city like a sheet spread out over a corpse. Fat crows perched on hibernating trees and cawed with menace from their lookouts. The mercury dropped and standing water turned to ice. Rivers and lakes hardened to a frozen slush. Winds born in Siberia lashed the exposed skin of the homeless or those who searched for food at Hamburg's ever-expanding black markets.

Heating fuel was hard to beg, borrow or steal because coal shipments from the Ruhr were always late. When the trains finally arrived with fresh supplies of coal, it didn't help matters much because most of the cargo had been plundered before the coal cars reached Hamburg. Some said the only heat being generated in Hamburg was in the bordellos along the Reeperbahn.

Water pipes froze and windows iced over from Lübeck to the working-class district of Altona. Apartment dwellers burned books in their kitchen stoves and sipped questionable moonshine purchased near mortuaries to stave off winter's chill. During the months known as the Hunger Winter, few thought or cared about culture – if you couldn't eat it or burn it, it was worthless. So it wasn't surprising that most of the city's frozen and desolate inhabitants were neither informed nor invited when the Hamburg Opera Company's performance of *The Marriage of Figaro* was held in a makeshift auditorium during the second week of January.

British occupying authorities sanctioned the concert as a gesture of goodwill to downcast high-brow Germans, who felt abandoned by civilisation. However, for most citizens, Mozart's return to Hamburg was treated with cynicism. Maria Edelmann scoffed at the news.

'The British won't feed us, but they'll stuff our souls with culture. How many calories are in an aria, I wonder?'

Friede believed that the opera gala's attendees were just Nazis dressed up as democrats. 'I imagine,' she said with disgust, 'that Germany's new entrepreneurs, the black marketeers, sat beside reformed Nazis and unrepentant communists. I bet each of them made a deal and sold out the German people during the performance. It doesn't matter whether it is a politician, egg-head or spiv; they are all painted from the same corrupt brush. They think Hamburg is their personal trough to stick their snout in and eat every last morsel.'

Not many days after the newly de-Nazified orchestra conductor was cheered by the well-heeled opera audience, a decree was issued by municipal authorities: the city's youth were to be put to work in factories owned by democratic capitalists.

The order was brief and to the point. Hamburg was rebuilding and all hands were needed to create a prosperous and democratic city. To that end, each young person not in school was required to register at the labour exchange located near the Rathaus, Hamburg's seat of municipal government. Failure to register, the order stated, would result in forfeiture of one's ration book. Letters were sent out to Hamburg's youth to reassure them that their future work assignments were to be based on skill and ability.

'What does this mean?' I asked, staring at the letter. It looked more like it had been written in the days of Hitler than in the year of liberation.

'It means it is over,' Friede responded angrily. 'I will be sent on to a work detail and they will destroy me there.'

'When do you have to report?'

'I have one week before I must appear at the labour exchange. So we'd better enjoy it, my love, because after that I will be property of the new Reich and the spivs that control the country.'

'Maybe it will be all right,' I said ignorantly.

'Sometimes you are so blind!' she screamed at me.

'Why? It just looks like they want to get everybody working again. What harm can there be in that?' I reasoned.

Friede walked to the other side of the kitchen and stared out from the French doors onto the snow-covered hills. She spoke more to herself than me. 'The bloody war interrupted my schooling. I have no skills for a proper job; I can't type, take shorthand, or even bake a cake. You know in this modern world it doesn't matter if I can recite Goethe by heart, it doesn't matter that I write and speak German like a university-educated person. My papers say I am uneducated. I will be assigned the lowest and most brutal work duties, where my only chance for advancement is to let the manager pinch my backside.'

'I won't let that happen,' I said emphatically.

Friede laughed and said, 'Harry, you work wonders down at the air base kitchen, but you are a tiny, tiny fish in a big ocean of sharks. You can't help me from this; no one can stop this from happening.'

The week before she was to report to the labour exchange, Friede and I spent our time together doing the usual: we made love, drank wine, and ignored the world outside.

Even though she was against it, I accompanied her to the labour exchange. On the U-Bahn into the city, we ate a breakfast of cold bacon sandwiches while famished commuters looked on in envy. From the Bahnhof, we walked south towards the Rathaus and the labour exchange.

It was a cold day and the temperature hovered at minus ten Celsius. Our breath stuck to our faces and Friede snuggled up close beside me to stay warm. Even though her body was near, she was emotionally distant. Friede had to battle her own demons and fears about her coming work assignment alone.

When we arrived, Friede sternly said: 'Whatever happens, promise me that you won't interfere with the outcome.' Reluctantly, I agreed.

Inside the giant labour exchange, we waited in a long queue with hundreds of other anxious young women each awaiting their uncertain assignment. Finally, our turn came and a man with thick spectacles at an information desk directed us to an office down the hall. There we were greeted by a plump and miserable woman, who told Friede: 'You must wait until your name is called for your interview. I can answer none of your questions, so don't bother asking me anything.'

There were no vacant seats so Friede and I stood close together and I observed her frustration and despair grow as we waited. After a while, Friede whispered angrily at me: 'See, I should have forbidden you to come with me. I am the only girl here with a Brit; I look like a complete traitor.'

I let her rant and fret, knowing that nothing I could say was going to change her mood.

After two hours of waiting, a woman with a pie-shaped face and drab wide slacks called out for Friede. I attempted to tag along to the interview room, but Friede stopped and scolded me.

'You're not going anywhere. I want you to stay here,' she said in a tone familiar to any dog that was told to wait outside a shop by his master. The dour woman led Friede behind a glass partition.

Feeling out of place, I went outside and stood on the steps of the building smoking a cigarette. Frozen, I watched young girls wrapped in greatcoats shuffle through the labour exchange doors where dubious new professions awaited them, created by occupation grants and shady industrialists. I didn't stay out in the cold for very long before returning to the office to wait for Friede. Around me there was a con-tinuous sound of telephones, typewriters and stamps being crushed against paperwork. It was another hour and a half before Friede emerged from behind the partition. She held in her hand a sheaf of papers and said to me, 'Let's get out of here. I need to get a coffee.'

We found a café near the government building. We took a table close to a cast-iron oven that had a few embers of coal burning in it to heat the entire restaurant. Friede barked out her order to the waiter for coffee and brandy. She fell silent and looked off into the distance until our drinks arrived. Friede quickly drank her brandy and requested another. She asked me for a cigarette, which I lit and handed to her.

'So what happened?' I asked.

Friede blew smoke from her mouth and began sipping on her second brandy.

'It was as I expected; nothing but rubbish. These new employment directives are just a sop to the occupiers. It is going to make the industrialists rich on slave labour, just like under Hitler.'

I took a sip from my drink and asked tentatively, 'What job were you assigned?'

Friede continued as if she didn't hear my question. 'This is just shit. It is only to prevent us from going out and protesting in the streets. It is to stop us from rising up against the occupation. These new work orders are to keep us cowed and happy with our starvation rations. This is our punishment for the war.' Friede looked directly into my eyes with a dismissive and disdainful gaze. 'The labour exchange has put me to work in a factory.'

'What sort of factory?' I asked reluctantly.

'The best kind,' she said, 'one that makes lampshades to sell to a city that has no electricity.' She laughed bitterly and repeated the word lampshade to herself. 'It's over,' she said.

'What's over?' I asked.

'Sometimes, you don't want to listen or understand me, do you?'

'Look,' I said, growing frustrated, 'I'm sorry they have forced you to work in this factory, but we can change that.'

'No you can't, Harry. Anyway, it is wrong to wriggle out of this new hell. In the past, I was saved too many times from my real fate. This is my retribution for being German; I can't escape it while everyone else is being punished.' Friede reached out to hold my hand and while stroking it, she said: 'I once asked you to promise me the moon. Now I am going to ask you to guarantee me something else.'

'Anything,' I said. 'I'll do anything.'

She let go of my hand and said without inflection, 'We must stop seeing each other. There is no future for us, only a miserable present because we can never marry.'

I was about to interrupt her when Friede dismissed my protest. 'Harry, we can't marry; that is the law. Those are the regulations of your country. How long is the RAF going to allow you to remain in Germany? It is wrong for either of us to hang on to a hope that is false, a lie. We can't go on like this, drinking wine, kissing, and forgetting the past or that we have no future together. You are nice; you are a kind man, Harry. Go home to England and find a girl back in Yorkshire who isn't as complicated as me. You have to make a life for yourself and so do I. It is just pointless to continue as friends. There is nothing we can look forward to but drinks in a café. Thank you for everything that you have done for me.'

Her voice was as icy as the wind outside. She stood up,

put on her gloves, and wrapped a scarf tightly around her neck. Standing beside the table, Friede said: 'I must ask you to stay away from me for ever.'

With those final words, Friede walked firmly out of the café and onto the frozen street. I lit another cigarette and stared at the brandy glass that had smudges of her lipstick around the rim.

CHAPTER 14

Spring

When spring came to Hamburg in 1946, it was a hard thaw. Bitter rain fell and made the city miserable, damp and dirty. Enthusiasm over winter's passing was dampened by the widespread hunger of the people. Daily ration allotments were still horrendous and the calorie intake was insufficient to sustain the average person. Only black market entrepreneurs looked healthy and wealthy compared to their grey-faced compatriots. It was little wonder that few Germans paid attention to the war crime trials under way in Nuremberg. Naturally, many just wanted these prosecutions to be over and done with, rather like pulling a diseased tooth.

'Sure, Göring, Ribbentrop and Hess are guilty. Send them all to the gallows,' the people said. 'But leave us ordinary Germans alone, we were just following orders.'

Gradually, the weather warmed and the days lengthened, but it did nothing to brighten my spirits. Instead, it depressed me because it reminded me too much of the year before, when hope and happiness lay at my feet, like garlands cast to victorious soldiers on parade. I was still raw from January when Friede broke off our affair. For weeks after Friede had fled the café, I looked for her like a dog run wild in the woods, but she wasn't going to let me find her.

It didn't matter where I searched because Friede had left no trail for me to follow. Most of her friends ignored me or reluctantly said that they had not spoken with her for some time. I went back to the restaurants we used to frequent and retraced my life with Friede. It was a futile hope that maybe I'd run into her. It never happened. I never caught sight of her. Even the waiters who remembered us shook their heads and politely said, 'Sorry, the Fräulein has not been in for weeks. Maybe you would like to meet my cousin. She is just as pretty.'

I purposely walked down Langenhorner Chaussee, hoping to confront Friede about our break-up, but I never saw her. One time, I even got up the courage and banged on Maria Edelmann's apartment door and asked the whereabouts of her daughter. Her mother said, 'Friede is not here, she is at work.'

I wanted to say, 'Tell her that I stopped by,' but her mother interrupted me: 'She doesn't want to see you any more, so it is best to respect her wishes.' I tried to leave some food rations for her, but Maria Edelmann declined and said, 'Please don't call again; it is embarrassing for everyone.' So I gave up and went back to the air base. I let my wounds fester for weeks.

Finally, my mate Sid grew tired of my moaning and told me, 'Cheer up, there's plenty of fish in the sea, especially in Hamburg. Let's get pissed.' So we did. Through that winter, I drank and went to parties and got stinking drunk as many times as it snowed, trying to forget my misery of the heart.

As I was hungover most days, I attended to my duties

at the airport telephone exchange reluctantly. My responsibilities were uncomplicated: I connected incoming or
outgoing telephone calls to our airport from the hundreds of other military bases across Europe and the UK.
It was a simple job made easier because we used captured
push-button German technology, which was superior to
our primitive patch cord system employed at RAF bases
in Britain.

It may have been more efficient, but it didn't change
the fact that it was numbingly dull. There was always an
incessant background hum from whirring teletype machines
or the thump of keyboards being heavily struck by one-
fingered typewriting impresarios. All around me, there was
the constant chatter of male telephone operators connecting
calls from one trunk to the next, with the politeness of a
lift operator.

On duty, my vocabulary was limited to: 'Fuhlsbüttel
BAFU, how may I direct your call?'

My fingers pushed buttons that connected one officer
with his wife in Surrey and another captain through to his
mistress in Elmsbüttel.

With Friede out of my life, I seriously considered pack-
ing it in and begging to be demobbed back to Halifax. By
this point, I was so jaded and heartbroken I thought I might
as well go and live in a glum flat and work as a serf in a wool
mill on a pound a week wages. When I griped to my mates,
Sid and Dave, they argued against my foolishness. 'Steady
on, lad, bide your time, things change and life isn't pleasant
for the serious-minded. We've got the day off and the sun is
shining, so let's get a couple of drinks at the Malcolm Club.'

I agreed and the three of us made our way from our airport base to the nearby club.

This social club was founded by the parents of Wing Commander Hugh Malcolm to honour their son who died in combat over enemy skies. Anywhere the RAF was stationed, a Malcolm was close by to provide refuge, relaxation, and tankards of beer or cider at a generous price.

Our Malcolm was located a short walk from base in a requisitioned restaurant that stood on the banks of a large artificial pond. We took advantage of the warm sunny day and drank our pints outside on benches overlooking the water. Out on the lake there was a flotilla of canoes, each being paddled by a soldier with a girl sitting at the bow. I ruefully said: 'I did that last year with Friede.'

'Shut it, Harry,' said Sid. 'We agreed no talk about girls. Pay the penalty, stand the next round.'

When I returned with the beer, Dave asked: 'Do you remember the chap from base that went mad last year?'

Sid shook his head, but I remembered. 'Wasn't he a mechanic or something?'

'That's right,' remarked Dave. 'He paddled a canoe out into the middle of the lake and scuttled it with a pocket knife.'

'He was unaware,' I added, 'that the reservoir was only waist-deep.'

Dave finished the story. 'The mad bugger was put on charges for not paying for the ruined canoe. All he wanted to do was end his life and he got clapped into irons for it.'

That afternoon we got seriously drunk and by tea time we had spent all our money. Leaving the Malcolm, we sang

RAF ditties and stumbled back towards camp, but lost our way. Instead of winding up at the gates of the aerodrome, we came upon an urban stable.

Dave suggested, 'Let's have a peek inside.'

'All right,' Sid and I both reluctantly agreed.

'We might be able to purloin some horses.'

'Steady on, Dave,' I said.

'What? You don't fancy a ride back to base? The women will go wild seeing you on a stallion. You'll look quite gallant.'

'I'll look a right tosser, you mean.'

It took the three of us to open the stable door because we were pissed and uncoordinated. Light filtered into the barn and suddenly I heard the sound of horses snorting and hooves scraping at their stalls. The stable was in immaculate condition. The floor was swept clean of debris. Dung was heaped in orderly piles ready to be collected and used as fertiliser.

'It's bloody marvellous,' I said to my mates. 'The Jerries are so fucking clean. Look at this place. It's neater than a lot of flops I've kipped in back home. Even the horse shit looks like it has been polished.'

Sid agreed and added, 'They're a sanitary lot, but dirty buggers when it comes to war. Remember how they left Holland? They didn't even bother to switch off the lights or close the door behind them.'

While Sid and I talked, Dave walked up to a brown quarter horse and began to stroke his mane. 'Now there's a good lad.'

'Where did you learn that?' I asked.

'My Granddad had a patch of land where he kept an old horse. I think he fancied himself a gentleman farmer with that old nag. Be a sport, Harry, and play waiter,' Dave said, while stroking the horse's flanks. 'They all look in need of a good tuck in.'

'What about us?' asked Sid. 'We haven't eaten since lunch.'

I fetched three buckets of oats for the horses. I handed them out to my friends. I brought mine over to a white mare that seemed anxious and famished. The horse stuck her mouth into the bucket and chomped on the fodder.

'Pity there's no bridle around,' said Dave.

Idiotically, I pointed to the wall where bridles and bits were hanging. Below the riding gear there should have been a written warning: 'A horse, especially a German horse, may not appreciate a foreign occupier as its master.'

Dave grabbed the equipment from the wall and expertly prepared the horses, calming them by speaking gently as if they were his children. He led two of them by their reins out of the stable and told me to do the same with the other horse.

I protested: 'Look, Dave, I'm not Nanette, the bareback rider of Barnum and Bailey fame. How am I supposed to get up on that beast without stirrups?'

Sid agreed. 'We're just playing silly buggers; let's get back to camp for tea.'

'Steady on, old chums,' Dave said. 'It will be no problem getting you lads up and down. Follow me and mind the fresh turds.'

We tagged behind and I muttered, 'Dave, since you're so

good with horses, perhaps you can get Hans to stop farting. He's got more wind than the base padre.'

Dave tethered off his horse and took mine and Sid's to a firm pile of bricks stacked neatly in the courtyard. 'Climb up onto that load of bricks. You can mount your horse from there. It will be like getting into bed.'

'What about when we're done?' Sid asked.

'For Christ's sake,' said Dave. 'Can't you lads be a bit more sporting? When we're done, we'll go back to the bricks and you can jump off from there. It's simple, now hop on.'

Reluctantly I obeyed and Sid followed my lead. I slipped onto the horse like Taras Bulba's halfwit brother. The horse held her footing while I nervously climbed on top. Off to the side, I noticed Dave effortlessly leap onto his bareback horse. My horse and Sid's stirred slowly away from the bricks.

'This is not too bad,' I said, and Sid nodded his head in agreement.

I was just getting comfortable in my role as horseman when suddenly the horse pricked her ears up. Her head reared up as if she had heard the bugle for the Epsom Derby. The horse charged out of the courtyard while I bounced on top of her. I looked back and saw Sid's horse charging in my wake. Dave's horse cantered at an even pace behind us.

Dave called out to us, 'Dig your knees into the horse's flank and pull back on the reins.'

'For Christ's sake,' I screamed at Dave, 'it took me three days to master driving a bloody Leyland lorry and it had a flipping clutch. Right now, I'm just going to hang on for fucking life.'

The three horses raced from the courtyard and out onto a side street. Their hooves made a heavy thundering noise on the cobblestones. We charged into the town's main square, skirting parked military vehicles and dodging slower-moving carts propelled by more temperate horses. I was out of breath from screaming at Dave to stop this ride before the horses bolted towards the heather-strewn fields in the countryside.

The horses circled the town square twice, as if the second time were a victory lap, then opened up at full throttle and bolted down a long open street. My stomach churned as if I was on a rough ferry crossing. Ahead of me, I heard Dave and Sid crying out with excitement. When I glanced up, they looked as happy as children riding on a merry-go-round in England.

Evidently, the horses knew these streets well and manoeuvred through them with practised precision; meanwhile I clamoured for Dave to stop this carnival ride gone berserk.

An MP on the roadside blew his whistle at us. He cried out as we rode past him at breakneck speed. 'What do you fatheads think you are up to? Stop this business at once!'

If I had had any means to reason with Bucephalus, I gladly would have complied, but this horse was its own master. Finally, the horses charged down Langenhorner Chaussee and out onto the common near the U-Bahn terminal. We sped across the open field and newly dug vegetable patches. In the distance, I even saw Friede standing with her mother on the apartment balcony. I hoped she didn't recognise me, but I was still overjoyed to catch sight of her for a brief and galloping second.

After twenty minutes, the horses tired and slowed their pace. With a snort, they returned to a languid trot and headed back towards the stables. We retraced our meandering way through the backstreets of Fuhlsbüttel. Bystanders, who only minutes ago had hidden fearfully behind shop doors, now derisively applauded and called out to us while standing on the roadside: 'Tommy, bravo Tommy …'

'Not exactly Christ's ride into Jerusalem,' I called out to the other two.

'Watch out, they may start throwing flowers at our triumphant arrival,' Sid responded.

At the entrance to the stable, we were met by the irate stable master. He was a man so cylindrical in shape he could have doubled as a postbox. Evidently, he was very comfortable with losing his temper. He upbraided us with all manner of curses in German. Finally, in utter frustration, he took his cap off and threw it to the ground in disgust at our actions.

Dave said to him, 'It was a delight to take your horses for a ride. As a show of goodwill for your troubles, take a packet of cigarettes, compliments of the Royal Air Force.'

Dave reached into his pocket and produced a packet of Capstans. The German greedily grabbed the pack. He seemed appeased – so much so, in fact, he tried to strike a bargain with Dave that would have given him unlimited horseback rides as long as he could supply a good number of cigarettes to the fat German.

My horse led me back to the pile of bricks, where I weakly dismounted from the creature. Sid and his horse returned to their own brick pile.

Dave dismounted from his horse as gracefully as a ballet dancer, looking refreshed and invigorated. Sid and I, however, looked green and bilious.

We swore never to go drinking with Dave again. 'It hurts too much,' I grumbled.

My testicles felt as if they had been twisted, bent and crushed beyond repair, like walnuts put into a paper bag and bashed with a hammer. I limped back to camp, cursing my friend and all horses in general. I made a solemn pledge that I would never in my life mount a horse or even a bike again.

CHAPTER 15

The sad-eyed girl at the Victory

As it does in April, it rained. The rain came down in sheets and at other times like mist, but it was steady and felt like it would never end. At night alone in my quarters, I chain-smoked and watched the rain splatter against my windowpane.

In my sister's monthly letter, she wrote: 'Life in Britain is shite, shite for work, shite for marriages and shite for relations between mothers and daughters.' She asked how my love affair with Friede was progressing. I replied with a lie and wrote that everything was smashing and my life had never been better.

Friends dropped by my room and asked, 'All right?'

I replied, 'Aces.'

Drinking and carousing deadened my feelings for Friede, dulled my wits, and blunted my nerves, but it was only a temporary relief to the ache. When off duty, I escaped into a world of unfulfilled expectations at the Victory dance club. Why not, I reasoned. May as well have a bit of fun and get what you give. I thought hanging out in dance halls was a bit like carbolic soap, a strong astringent to scrub love from my hands like it was muck. Unfortunately, it achieved the opposite and I felt grimier each time I returned from the club. The more I tried to drown my loitering funk with drink, loud music and conversations with nameless girls, the more my unhappiness stuck to me.

There was a predictable pattern to each of my nights at the Victory. Before I headed out, I vigorously shined my boots and boasted to anyone in earshot that the tips reflected the moon's gleam. I kneaded generous amounts of Brylcreem into my scalp so that no hair shifted from its brushed position. My pressed uniform snapped to my body and I was ready to join the queue in front of the Victory.

No matter the time spent in preening or practising suave pick-up lines – I had little success with the opposite sex at the Victory. Not being able to dance and afraid to try, I wasn't able to keep a girl's attention for long. So any woman who joined my table didn't linger for longer than a moment. The Fräuleins tapped their feet to the rhythm of the drummer on stage. They fidgeted with the contents of their purse and pretended to hear my wooing words over musicians performing Benny Goodman covers with counterfeit enthusiasm. Normally, the young woman politely finished her drink and said, 'Are you sure you don't want to dance?' And I'd respond: 'Sorry, gammy leg, from the war, you know.'

Embarrassed, she'd smile and promise, 'I'll be back shortly.'

Within minutes of her departure, I'd see her jitter-bugging with an American or another airman from camp. Loneliness and self-pity twitched over my body as I watched them dance. Whisky and water or strong lager quickly numbed my solitude.

Most nights at the Victory club were like that for me: lots of whisky and lots of German girls who blew me off once they realised I didn't dance and wouldn't buy them a champagne cocktail. It didn't take long for the varnish to thin on my expectations of love or sex at the Victory. I decided it was a waste of my money and my time to prowl for birds in a club that tried every night to re-create the joy and relief we had found on the day the war ended in Europe.

It was on my last visit to the club, where sobriety was a sin and prudence a crime, that I met a woman who looked as sad as me. She approached my table and said, 'I don't want to dance. I just want to rest my feet. Do you mind?'

Her name was Sonya and she was very beautiful. She claimed she was 30, but I think she was probably older. I began to date her because it seemed the easiest way to clear Friede out of my head for good. In a strange way I liked Sonya because she was totally uninterested in me, except for my money and the rations I provided her. The woman also had rules for our relationship. It was made clear to me that if I wanted to remain her boyfriend I was to obey her strange whims.

'Whatever you want, darling; if I can only see you on Tuesdays and Thursdays, that is fine by me,' I said without much enthusiasm.

Sonya lived in the posh part of Hamburg near the Alster. So I found her requests for generous supplies of cigarettes and tinned coffee unusual, even suspicious. I had presumed this well-to-do neighbourhood was insulated from the troubles of total war and rationing.

Outside of kissing and some uncomfortable

hand-holding, we were never physical with each other. Sonya didn't want to pursue sex and I didn't push the matter. I tried to get her to come out with me to restaurants or the park, but she refused.

'We can only meet at my home,' she said, while taking a packet of coffee from my duffle bag and disappearing with it into another room. 'I prefer to spend our time alone,' she explained.

It looked like she also preferred to spend her time alone with my Maxwell House coffee because she never offered me anything from her larder but tepid cups of camomile tea.

While in my company, Sonya generally sat morosely in a wingback chair and stared aimlessly at anything but me. After much silence, she'd ask me to pour her some wine. She didn't even have a gramophone to drown out her heavy sighs.

After a month of visits, I was overcome by curiosity and asked, 'What do you do with all the cigarettes and coffee I bring you? You're not trading it for food because you look as thin as a sheet.'

'Must you always ask so many questions?' She tried to evade answering with another sigh, but I smelled a strong scent of cigarettes coming from her bedroom.

'Why is it that your house always smells of cigarettes even when we're not smoking?'

'I don't know what you mean,' she said defensively.

'Do you live alone?' I asked.

'Of course,' Sonya replied.

'So there isn't someone in your bedroom taking a fag break?' I asked suspiciously.

She got up from her chair and moved towards the bedroom door. 'There is no one in there.'

'Do you have a cat, then, who has taken to smoking Kensingtons, because I distinctly smell a burning cigarette?'

Almost hysterical, Sonya screamed, 'You are such a fool and I think it is time you go.'

She grabbed my coat and pushed me out the door and asked, 'Are we still on for Thursday?'

I yelled back at her, 'You're barmy!'

'Remember to bring more cigarettes and coffee when you come again,' she responded.

I went back to my quarters in Fuhlsbüttel swearing under my breath that I wasn't going to see Sonya any more. She could go hang. Thursday, however, intervened and I had nothing planned. So I returned to her house and Sonya wasn't surprised by my arrival, despite my harsh words at our last encounter.

'Did you bring the cigarettes and coffee?' she asked anxiously.

'Yes,' I said irritably. 'Is that all I am to you, a corner shop?'

Sonya responded with little eagerness and purred, 'You can sleep with me if you want, I don't mind at all.' She began unbuttoning her blouse.

'I don't think you understand me,' I said naively. 'Sure, I'd like to sleep with you, but not because I gave you cigarettes. We'd have to at least like each other a little or this is just all wrong.'

'Have it your way,' Sonya said. 'If you want to complicate things, go ahead and complicate them. See, now I won't sleep with you; are you happy? But I still need the cigarettes and coffee,' she said, while doing up the buttons on her blouse.

'Hold on,' I said, 'this is just nuts. What are you saying? Why do you need so many cartons of cigarettes and tins of coffee? I should think you are doing just fine. Look where you live. You obviously come from money and you are exceptionally beautiful, so I don't understand your desperation for black market goods. You must still have good connections around town.'

Before I was able to finish my sentence, the bedroom door opened. Out came a man wearing a suit two sizes too big for him. He was unshaven and I guessed he was a little younger than Sonya.

'What the hell?' I stood up, thinking I was about to be robbed.

'Sonya, you'd better tell him,' the man told her. The woman started to cry quietly. The man put his arm around Sonya and comforted her as he spoke to me. 'May I call you Harry?' he asked. 'I feel as if I already know you.'

'Have you been in that room every time I've been here?' I asked.

'I am afraid so.'

'What the hell were you doing in there?'

'I am the reason she needs the cigarettes and coffee from you.'

'Oh Christ,' I said in an irritated voice. I lit a cigarette and blurted out, 'You're on the lam and hiding from us.'

'Let's just say I have no papers and leave it at that,' he said.

Sonya stopped crying and interjected. 'Hans is my boy-friend and I love him, but I can't get him a ration book without an ID card. The cigarettes and coffee along with the jewellery I sold were going to help us get out of Hamburg and start a new life somewhere else.'

'So you go around to the dance clubs looking for soldiers who will give you extra rations? That's your plan? Fleece soldiers so your boyfriend can eat and live underground, undetected by our military? How many boyfriends does it take to keep Hans fed?'

'Several,' she replied tearfully.

'Blimey, both of you are real pieces of work. I don't know who is dirtier in this whole sorry business. Hans, you are a real gent letting your woman do all the dirty work so you can stay out of trouble. My advice to you is to turn yourself in to the authorities.' He was about to answer when I told him: 'Forget it, mate, don't tell me. I don't want to know. From this point onwards, I don't want to know anything.'

I made my way to the door and Sonya said, 'Are you going?'

'Yes.'

'Are you ever coming back?'

'Not bloody likely.'

'Please don't tell anyone about us.'

I never shopped Sonya and Hans out. I was too ashamed that I had been taken in by sad eyes and a hard-luck story in the most expensive part of Hamburg when I came from the lowest end of Halifax. My discomfort at being Sonya's dupe soon dissipated. I didn't much care for her and I thought I was well enough rid of her and her sad eyes pleading for coffee and fags. I kept the story to myself because I knew if Sid or Dave or anyone else got wind of my stupidity, I would have been base fool for the year.

In May, Sid asked: 'What happened to Sonya?'

'She wasn't my type and like you said, there are plenty of fish in the sea,' I responded.

'Too right, too right,' said Sid. 'Fancy a beer?'

'No, I am going to Planten un Blomen to see if I can clear my head of bloody women.'

I never got to the park. I never got to clear my head of bloody women. Right after I left the U-Bahn station in the downtown core, I saw Friede on the other side of the street.

CHAPTER 16

The girl from
the lampshade factory

I t had been four months since I had last seen her. At first, I wasn't sure if it was Friede or my imagination just winding me up. But then a surge like an electric shock sparked through my body and told me the person across the way was Friede. She was walking towards the Dammtor Bahnhof and one thing was definite: her looks had drastically changed since we last met.

Her hair was tied up at the back in the manner of a factory girl. She was thinner and looked as frail as straw. Friede walked timidly as if she was going into a pool of water with an uncertain current. Everything about her was different, even her clothing. Instead of a fashionable dress, she now wore grubby worker's overalls covered in dark paint. Friede looked like every other German in the city: beaten, preoccupied, and disillusioned by hunger and a questionable future.

I darted across the road to get to her side of the street and almost collided with a jeep. Until we got to the Dammtor Bahnhof, I followed at a discreet distance. Inside, Friede struggled towards the U-Bahn's platform. As usual, it was hot inside the terminal and packed with factory workers and rubble clearers waiting for their connection to go home. Friede's head was bowed, fixed on the concrete as if in contemplation or empty prayer, or just because she was too tired to look at another commuter.

Loudspeakers declared the arrival of another train. Above me, the cast-iron ceiling vault was still exposed, naked to the elements because glass enclosures were a luxury for a city on its knees. I turned my eyes downwards and away from the pigeons darting through the uncovered steel ribs of the Bahnhof. I looked towards Friede imprisoned in the crowd and didn't know whether to follow her or let her be and let us be.

I watched her slip anonymously onto a U-Bahn car. Impetuously, I thought: to hell with it, better jump right back into the muck. At the very last moment, while a train guard whistled the all-clear, I hopped onto her car.

Friede stood at the far end of the compartment from me. She held on to a vertical metal bar in front of a wooden seat occupied by a thin, ragged woman whose mouth was ajar as if rigor mortis had already set in. Friede swayed with the motion of the train, like cargo not completely secured down. By the time we were half-way to Fuhlsbüttel, I had edged my way from one end of the car to the other and now stood right behind her.

There was a strong chemical odour boiling off her clothes. It smelled something like turpentine and copper. Sweat and dirt glistened in her hair and ran down the nape of her neck. I wondered, if she turned around, how I was going to explain my reasons for travelling on this train.

Oh hello, fancy meeting you on the U-Bahn, after all this time. I'm brilliant. How about you?

A series of phrases I'd learned from B-movies, each one more of a cliché than the last, swirled in my head. I knew if she turned around and asked me to explain myself, quoting Trevor Howard in *Brief Encounter* wasn't going to work on Friede. I worried that she'd be cross with me for following her. Christ, I thought, now I've done it, she will hate me or start a scene. People will stare at me and I will look the proper ass.

For a moment, I wanted to sneak off the train, disappear into the crowd, and hope she never knew that I'd been running after her. I suppose my thoughts leaked out of me like an ice cube melting on a counter-top, because Friede twitched to my presence. She cleared her throat and adjusted her purse. She kept her back to me but spoke. 'Harry?'

'Yes.'

'I see you still like staring at my back,' she said in a whisper.

'No, no,' I said in apology, 'nothing like that at all. I was just ...'

Friede interrupted my insincere apologies. 'I think this time you might beat me in the game we once played.'

'What game was that?' I asked, confused.

'Don't you remember? We'd run between train cars and see who got left behind at the station.' The lights overhead flickered as our train ducked into a tunnel.

I said, 'Well, I'm not much good at sports. So why don't we call it a draw?'

As we travelled underground, I saw our faces reflected in the window. I smiled, but I think it was more a grimace and hoped she wouldn't notice the difference.

'How've you been?' I asked tentatively in formal German, reserved for strangers and superiors.

'I can tell you one thing for sure; my feet have known happier times because right now, they ache beyond description. As for the rest of me, it wouldn't say no to a decent cup of coffee and a good night's sleep.' Friede shifted her feet and brushed her hand against her hair and fell silent.

Was this all that was going to be spoken between us, I wondered. When our train emerged from the tunnel and into daylight, with her back still facing me, she asked, 'And how have you been?'

'Me, I've been all right, busy you know, with work at the base and being out with the mates,' I said, lying brazenly and badly. 'Mind you, I've missed you some,' I added, trying to dismiss my false bravado.

At Ohlsdorf, the last stop before Fuhlsbüttel, the train pulled out from the station with a sudden surge. Friede slipped backwards onto me. For the first time in a long while, our bodies touched. Quickly, she righted herself and broke away from me like a balloon let out of a child's hand.

Over the clack of rail ties, she said, 'I missed you too, Harry, but what's a girl to do?'

We arrived at the Fuhlsbüttel terminal and the door beside her opened up. She said, without looking back, 'I will see you later, Harry.'

She stepped off the train and into the sunlight and I trailed behind her.

'Can you just stop for a second?' I begged.

'I don't want you to see me like this.'

'I don't care.'

'Well, I do mind you seeing me like this. If you want to talk to me, come by the little café near my mother's apartment, around seven tonight. We can talk then.' Friede skirted away and disappeared down a set of stairs that took her to street level.

I rushed back to camp and cleaned myself up for our rendezvous. During my preparations, I don't know whether I hoped for an explanation for her leaving me or a resumption of our love affair. Either way, I felt awkward and raw from our time apart.

I arrived at the café early. Friede was late and didn't show until almost half past seven. Although she still looked tired, any traces of her afternoon proletarian demeanour had vanished. She wore a breezy summer dress that was a size too large for her. The necklace I had given to her for her birthday dangled around her neck. Her hair was no longer tied up, but fell luxuriant to her shoulders. I also noticed that her leg ulcers had returned from lack of vitamins. I stood to greet her and said, 'You look fantastic.'

She touched my cheek lightly and whispered, 'Hello.'

She smelled of rose water and fresh air, unlike the afternoon when she was covered in industrial grime.

When the waiter arrived, Friede ordered cake, coffee and brandy. She ate it ravenously and excused herself. 'I am sorry. I haven't eaten since lunch at the factory.'

'Would you like some more cake?' I asked.

'No, but perhaps I could have some more coffee with a touch of brandy. May I have one of your good cigarettes?'

I lit it for her. 'I missed your good manners,' she noted

and swept some stray strands of hair that had fallen across her face. 'No one at the factory or anyone around me has the time for good manners. It is all about getting rations, or getting out of the manager's roving eye.'

The brandy came and she said, 'You are going to get me drunk.'

I smiled and replied, 'As long as I can get drunk with you.'

Friede sighed. 'If only that were possible, but five o'clock comes early and it is brutal work. I think it would kill me if I had to do a shift hungover.'

I thought this was almost like old times. Yet when I looked into her eyes, I understood a lot had changed between us. We were now separated by the culture of victory and defeat. No one was spared, except those with connections to officials who could offer employment deferrals.

Friede noticed my meditation and said, 'Go on then. You want to know about my new life and how horrible it is, so please, ask me.'

I hesitated for a second and said, 'I don't know if I want to find out what you've been up to.'

'Come on,' she urged me. 'You were always so curious about my life during the war. You may as well know what my life is like in post-war Hamburg, post-Harry.'

So over the next hour and a bit, she told me about her new life as a factory worker for a questionable industrialist.

'It is ironic,' she said, 'but my factory is near the dock-lands. It is not too far from Uncle Henry's old office, where he used to do all of his big tobacco deals during the war.'

The factory where Friede worked wasn't as grand as

Uncle Henry's office block. It was a single-storey building that had somehow survived the bombing and was used as it had been under the Nazis, for light industrial assembly and storage.

'I will never understand,' she said contemptuously, 'how the British dropped so many bombs on this city and missed blowing up this factory. It isn't even a real factory; after all, we only assemble ugly lampshades, not Volkswagens.'

Her factory, Friede explained, was licensed by the German civilian authorities to assemble lampshades for commercial sale.

'I don't even know if some other part of this company makes the actual lamps for the shades. Anyway, the owner doesn't give a damn because he is well taken care of by the British.'

I sipped on my drink and said, 'I don't see how the Brits are interested in some small-time company.'

'Harry,' she said without malice, 'you are sometimes such an innocent. The British think that businessmen like him keep young Germans occupied and out of trouble with mindless tasks. Hard work for rotten wages, they believe, will keep us from grumbling about our pitiful rations and living conditions. No one can riot in the streets if they are forced by law to work in factories run by corrupt capitalists. I am also sure that some of the Brits are even getting large gifts from these industrialists as a thank you for all of the start-up money wasted on murky businessmen.'

According to Friede, the owner of her factory was given sacks of cash by the military government to form his company. Apparently, money was always available no matter how stupid or unprofitable the businesses, as long as the owners were on sufficiently good terms with the British.

Stabbing at her cake with a fork, Friede continued. 'To get money from the British, the spivs make sure their shoes don't smell of Nazism. The owner,' Friede added sarcastically, 'Herr I-am-a-big-shot-now, once came out onto our factory floor. He gave us girls a speech about how his company was rebuilding Hamburg.' The factory owner said he had lost his old business under the Nazis. 'It was some sob story or another about how his loss was our gain because we are now part of this great enterprise to make lampshades.' She laughed and continued. 'I am sorry he lost his business under Hitler, but does that make it right that our weekly wages barely pay for a loaf of bread?'

Friede admitted she didn't know or care much about her employer's life or his problems with the Nazis. It was black and white for her because she was certain that her boss was out to line his own pockets. In Friede's description, the factory owner believed that cronyism and democracy were identical and that his stealing from the purse of Britain and the dead victims of Hitler wasn't only justified, it was progress. Friede thought the industrialist was going to grift his way to a nice house in Switzerland.

'Harry, this I can promise you; he is not going to thank Britain or Germany for his good fortune.'

'I am sure some of these new businesses are on the up and up,' I said, with not much conviction.

'Of course there are honest men in Hamburg,' Friede responded, 'but they are hard to find even in daylight.'

These new German capitalists, according to her, were

all in on the deal to profit from the chaos around them. 'They are all hacks and friends of the civilian government,' she said, lighting another cigarette. Friede got a little drunk and started to giggle after her third brandy.

'Where I work, I call it a sweatshop rather than a factory.'

Friede described her working day, which did sound pretty horrible and pointless. Wire frames were sheathed with a canvas covering. Paint was applied and then Friede had to coat the fabric with asbestos as a fire retardant.

'The dust gets in my eyes and in my mouth and I cough up horrible things after a day at work. Do you see now, Harry, what it is like in Germany without connections? Our great Hamburg labour council couldn't care less about me. I am just a worker for a corrupt factory owner who manufactures lampshades. Our city doesn't need more light to see they are hungry. It's crazy; we can't even make lampshades in different colours. All of ours are the same bloody colour: hideous green,' she said in despair. 'In five years, everyone in Hamburg is going to have an ugly green lampshade. Maybe in Bremen they are making red lampshades and in Frankfurt yellow,' she said sarcastically.

She finished speaking and played with the remnants of her cake. Friede looked away from me and told me, 'I always feel so tired and useless now.'

The hurt, anger and self-pity I'd endured when Friede left me simmered away like margarine on a skillet. I knew I hadn't stopped loving her, but I also felt helpless holding on to that love.

Her experiences over the last several months left me

hollow because they led me back to the hopelessness of my childhood. It was something I knew since I was weaned off my mother's breast: whether the love is strong or weak, it cannot survive hunger, it cannot endure the immutable harshness that life showers upon individuals too poor to have connections or luck. For the destitute, death is the only intervention that ends despair.

At 23, I finally understood that this was how my father must have suffered when he couldn't feed his children in the Great Depression and faded out of our lives. I wasn't sure what I could do for Friede. What was I going to offer her, words? I didn't want to abandon her to handling dangerous chemicals for pennies a week. But I was just a radio operator, a cavalier switchboard receptionist. I was just a young man who knew right from wrong. But I was no match against black marketeers and dodgy industrialists. Naively, that night, I offered her hope. It was a lifeline that was sure to snap when faced with the morning's cold reality.

'Give me the address of this factory. Tomorrow I will meet you there for lunch and get you discharged from that miserable place.'

Friede laughed and said, 'It will never happen. This is beyond you.'

'If I do this, can we see each other again?' I asked.

She touched my hand. 'I don't think you can do anything for me, Harry. But you can try. Don't worry if you fail because I still have many feelings for you.'

'I love you,' I said impetuously. 'It hurts, God damn it, when you're not around me, when you left me.'

'Harry, I never stopped loving you, but I learned from

my mother that you can't live off love. Now I must go,' she said, and on a piece of paper she wrote down the factory's address for me.

'If you really want to try and help me, meet me at the front of the building at 12:30. It is when we take our lunch break.'

'Who should I talk to at the factory?'

'It won't be the owner because he is out spending his money. His toady is a man named Papp. He is a pig who is always trying to touch the girls' bottoms.' Friede let go of my hand and added, 'I'll see you tomorrow.' She walked out of the café without looking back.

I settled the bill and returned to camp. That evening, I worked out a plan to free Friede from her dangerous factory job.

CHAPTER 17

The Rathaus, where dreams are painted the colour of money

The following morning, I asked my mates Sid and Dave to come with me to the plant. I needed them to help set Friede free from her hazardous job at the lampshade factory.

'Who do you think we are – the three bleeding musketeers?' asked Sid.

'More like the Marx Brothers,' replied Dave.

'Right,' said Sid in a conspiratorial voice. 'Since there's nothing more exciting to do today than break a few laws and probably a few heads, I'm all for busting your bird out from the evil German's factory. So we may as well get on with it,' he concluded. 'I've got one question, before we go. If we do liberate Friede, you owe me big. Can you can get her friend Gerda to go out with me?'

'I'll see what I can do.'

Dave said: 'Don't bother to get me a German lass, you can just get me a pint and we're square.'

'What about getting us a jeep from the motor pool?' I asked.

'That will be two pints,' he replied.

We set out for the factory just before noon. Dave drove, I rode shotgun, and Sid lounged in the back like a pasha out for a trip around his domain. When we pulled out of the camp gates, Dave asked: 'So what's your plan?'

'I've got none except for you guys to look tough and I'll try to bribe her manager.'

'It'll never bloody work,' they both said.

'Say, Harry,' Dave asked, 'once you bust Friede out of the lampshade factory, what are you going to do then? You still can't marry her. The law says you can't bring any Fräuleins home to England. Anything you take from Germany has got to fit in yer kit bag.'

'I know, I know,' I said. 'It's a real bugger. But I've heard the Labour government is thinking of changing the law.'

'At least Prime Minister Attlee isn't a shit like Churchill,' said Sid.

'What do ya mean?' Dave responded sarcastically. 'Winston got me this plum job.'

'That's what I'm talking about,' said Sid. 'Winnie thought we was all right when we fought them on the beaches. It was when we wanted to make love to them by Brighton Rock that his gang said no bloody way.'

I agreed. 'With the Tories, it's "Right, lads, tea break's over; you've done yer part and beat Hitler. Shut yer gob. Get back to Britain and get back to work at the end of a bloody shovel."'

'Go on,' Dave said sceptically, 'where did you hear this news about his nibs letting us marry foreigners?'

'I got it from one of the officers on base. I was on shift at the telephone exchange when I placed his call to some other muck in Lübeck. I left the line open by mistake and got to hear an earful. He told his mate that Parliament is going to change the law prohibiting soldiers marrying foreign nationals.'

'I guess too many blokes were putting girls up the spout or falling in love with exotic beauties from Belgium and France,' Sid added.

'Don't know and it doesn't matter,' I replied. 'They can be up the Khyber, but it's not the trump card for getting the marriage approved. The couple has to demonstrate a mutual affection for each other and the proposed missus can't be a security risk to the nation.'

'If those conditions were applied to couples wanting to get hitched in Nottingham, no one would be married,' said Dave. 'Starting a month before marriage, everyone begins to hate each other.'

'Till death do them part,' replied Sid.

'Anyway,' I continued, 'the officers weren't too happy about it. The new law includes all serving personnel, not just NCOs and officers, but enlisted men as well.'

'Makes 'em think they got rights or something,' Sid yelled from the back seat of the jeep.

'That's all right for you then, Harry,' Dave said, after blasting his horn as we passed a slow-moving horse-drawn carriage.

'Maybe,' I responded. 'These officers were really browned off and said that "Blighty already had enough foreigners but to add Germans into the mix was going to turn the island into a mongrel's paradise."'

When we arrived at Friede's workplace, Dave parked the jeep by its front entrance. The factory was sandwiched between two destroyed buildings. Out front, I saw Friede and her co-workers dressed in smocks looking dusty and grey.

Sid said, 'Jesus wept, Harry, they look a sad lot. Maybe after tea we can bust some waifs out of a match factory.'

'It's the orphans next, Sid,' I answered. 'Remember to get your priorities straight.' I jumped out of the jeep and my two friends followed suit.

I walked up to Friede, but she gave me a cold look as if to tell me not to be too familiar with her while there were other workers around.

Hastily, she said: 'Our break is almost over. I was afraid that last night was just a dream and you were not coming. I have to go back inside now. Wait outside until all the girls have gone back to work and then you can talk to Papp, my manager.' I nodded my head in agreement.

She added: 'I don't think anything good will happen, but I will cross my fingers for luck anyway.' Friede slunk back into the factory with her fellow workers.

'What's the story?' asked Dave.

'Give them a couple of minutes,' I replied.

'Then what?' asked Sid.

'We charge in and see if her manager will take my bribe and let her go.'

'He'd be a blockhead not to take the coffee,' said Sid.

'As long as we don't end up in the glasshouse, Harry,' Dave warned. 'Do what you must, but try to keep us out of the lock-up.'

A sign was posted on the factory's front door that read in German: 'Unauthorised personnel are forbidden to enter.'

'What does it say?' Dave asked.

'It says welcome.' I pushed open the heavy fire door and we walked inside to discover a nineteenth-century workshop. This netherworld was feebly lit from distant sunlight that shone through several broken windows near the ceiling. A fog of dust and paint drifted like a chemical apparition around the structure. Some of it clung to my uniform while the rest sank to the concrete floor. I noticed that my polished black boots were prematurely greyed from particles scattered on the ground. There was a strong chemical odour that burned my nostrils and made my eyes water. 'Fuck,' I said to no one in particular.

'Oi,' Sid said, 'look around. It's only birds working in this factory.'

He was right. There were about 30 females labouring in the building. Their work area was divided up into various stations of assembly. On one long table, eight women stretched fabric across flimsy wire frames. At another table, women painted the lampshades a green hue that resembled algae on a dead pond.

It was at the final and most dangerous work station that Friede and several other girls earned their meagre wages. With thin paintbrushes, they applied a noxious asbestos fire retardant resin to the one-size-fits-all lampshades. Inside the building, the air was so polluted that the women hacked and spat bits of paint and chemical residue onto the floor. This wasn't a factory; it was a workhouse run with the cruel inefficiency of Oliver's Twist's orphanage. It was a business enterprise with one motivation: to profit through exploitation and substandard working conditions. There was nothing here that redeemed either the owner or the workers; it was pure and simple slavery.

At the far end of the factory floor, I saw Friede. She was dragging a heavy sack over to her work table. The bag was ripped and its contents sprayed into the air like feathers and landed in her hair and across her face. 'This is a fucking nightmare,' I hollered.

My two friends agreed and said, 'Go get the bastard, Harry.'

Friede looked towards me and pointed to an office door. It was her manager Papp's lair.

With Sid and Dave in tow, I marched over and barged into the office without knocking. Inside, Herr Papp sat behind a desk, smoking a cigarette and reading a newspaper. He was about 40 with cauliflower ears, a close-cropped haircut and small colourless eyes. His face was lost in the eclipse of a five o'clock shadow. His grubby features aptly reflected his inner grime.

'Papp,' I hollered. He wasn't startled when he looked up at us crowded into his room. He seemed to expect this treatment by others who were in power.

'What?' he grumbled.

'I need you to release one of your workers from her contract with this company.'

He laughed and demanded, 'Under whose authority?'

'Mine,' I said.

He laughed even louder. 'Who the fuck are you?' he asked with incredulity.

Dave screamed, 'Please, let me hit him Harry.'

'No, you can't,' I said, and then yelled out to the

manager: 'Herr, Papp, your company is unfairly treating its workers. I demand that this cease immediately. I also request that one of your workers be released from their contract with this company.'

Papp got up from his desk and moved towards me, his cigarette hanging from his lip like a birth mark. He stood in front of me, smoke pouring from his homemade fag.

'What is this to you?' he asked, and then angrily demanded, 'Where are your orders?'

'I've got none,' I said.

'Then you are wasting my time. No papers, no worker, fuck off.'

'I have coffee,' I said.

Papp pulled the wet, yellow cigarette stump from his mouth and began to contemplate the offer. 'How much coffee do you have?'

'Two kilos; that can buy you a lot of stuff on the black market,' I told him.

'That is a great deal of coffee,' he noted greedily as if considering the trade.

With more friendliness in my voice, I said, 'Come on, one worker for two kilos of coffee. That is a fair trade and it's not going to harm your operation. You would never miss one girl, would you?'

Papp laughed like a man who has just seen a child stumble from their bike. 'Me, I wouldn't miss any of these bitches if they fell off the edge of the world. But,' he added, 'the big man who owns this factory might have something to say about it. Especially since those cows out on the floor make him money. The boss likes money and he counts his geld every day. My chief knows what he is worth down to the last pfennig and he's not going to be cheated out of anything that is his.'

Papp walked past us and opened his door. He pointed towards the factory floor outside. He said: 'Take a look around; the government pays my boss to make those bitches work. He's paid handsomely for the shit those girls make in this factory. One less girl is one less lampshade being produced, which is like stealing a mark from the boss's wallet. Verstehen?'

'Who's your fucking boss, the Cyclops in *Ulysses*?' I asked.

'Go away,' said Papp, returning to his desk.

'I'm not going anywhere,' I said with irritation.

'Look, Englishman, you are nobody. So fuck off and get out of my office before I call the military police.'

I would have lunged at him, but Sid jumped in my way and told me, 'Time to leave, we'll cook this squarehead's goose another day and wipe the smile off his flipping mug.'

My two friends dragged me out of the office as I screamed, 'I'll be back, you bastard!'

As we left the factory, Friede stuck her head up from her work bench and gave me a sad and resigned look.

When we returned to the jeep, Dave said, 'Well, that's it then. We may as well head back to camp. Sorry, Harry, better luck next time.'

On our way back I sat in the front seat of the jeep, sullen and angry. I felt I had caused Friede more harm by returning into her life than if I had just left her alone. Dave drove through Hamburg's downtown core.

'Why are you going this way?' I groaned.

'Just trying to cheer you up. It's a longer way home, but maybe we can think of a way of getting your Friede out of that hellhole.'

'Let's just get back to base,' I said forlornly.

My mind was drowned in anger and self-pity. My thoughts didn't clear until we drove by Hamburg's Rathaus, their seat of civic government.

'Hold on,' I said, 'I have an idea.' I would plead my case to the city's Burgermeister to release Friede from her indentured employment. My friends weren't too pleased with this new scheme.

'Harry, we're all going to be on charges,' Dave said.

'Why are you going to involve the bleeding mayor?' Sid asked.

'The mayor helped enact this new work regulation with the occupation authorities. Maybe he can change it for one of his citizens if I plead with him. I'll keep you two out of it, don't worry.'

Dave let me out of the jeep at the front of the municipal building. Before they drove off, I added: 'I'll catch up with you later. If anybody asks me about today, I'll say I was alone. So no worries, mates, I'll keep schtum. If it's my head, it's my head, but you two aren't going to end up in stir.'

The jeep drove off. I walked nervously towards the Rathaus. It was built in a neo-Renaissance style to reflect the power, wealth and influence of the town burghers, the shipping magnates, the rich bankers and brokers. It was an impressive edifice and any Venetian Doge would have gladly taken it as his palace.

When I walked through the portico, I was overcome by the building's opulence in contrast to the factory's squalor. Inside these walls, bureaucrats and patricians played out games of power, influence and double dealing, on a Herculean scale. It was here and at British HQ that the lives of millions of Germans were settled over a handshake or a cigarette and sometimes just a wink and a nod.

I grew unsettled as I walked across the immense Italian marble floors, feeling dwarfed by destiny. Papp was right. I was nobody. Unnerved, I was still determined not to show it. I marched towards a reception desk like I was an air commodore. A pretty blonde secretary looked up and smiled at me. She asked the nature of my business, in English.

Without hesitating, I replied: 'I am here to see the Burgermeister; my name is Harry Smith.'

She looked down at an appointment book and replied in a friendly tone of voice, 'Burgermeister Petersen is expecting you.'

'Expecting me?' I said with some hesitation.

'Yes, you are on the list of approved visitors,' she replied, reading from the appointment book. 'Here it is: H. Smith, from Flensburg. You are a bit early but that is all right, the Burgermeister can see you now.'

Considering that there was another Smith on his way to see the mayor, I thought it was best to get to him as quickly as possible and get out of this government building before being arrested. The secretary asked if I knew my way around the building and I replied that I didn't.

She left her desk and said, 'Follow me.'

I was led up an elegant marble staircase to the second floor, which housed the offices for the civilian government functionaries. The corridor to the mayor's office was long and panelled in heavy oak. The floors echoed from the sound of my boots and the secretary's shoes clapping against their polished surface. Carved busts of former senators and statesmen stuck on pedestals glared at me in stony silence. The secretary looked at me and asked, 'Is this your first time here?'

'Yes.'

'Did you know that the Rathaus is bigger than your Buckingham Palace?'

'No,' I replied, 'and I can assure you that it is definitely not my palace.'

The secretary laughed and said, 'We have arrived.' She knocked on an ornate double door and escorted me inside. Behind a mahogany desk sat Rudolf Petersen, former shipping magnate, exile from Hitler's Germany, and now the British-appointed civilian leader of Hamburg.

At the moment the secretary announced me, Petersen got up from his leather chair and crossed over to greet me with a handshake. He dismissed the secretary and said, 'I think Trudi has confused you with someone else I was expecting.'

'Yes. I am sorry for the mix-up.'

'Do you have business with me?' he asked kindly.

'I believe I do.'

'Well then, please have a seat. My office is always open to the RAF.'

The mayor first began by asking me where I was stationed and where I came from in Britain. When I told him I was from Yorkshire, his eyes lit up like a birthday candle.

'I know the moors very well and spent many a happy time there. You are very lucky to have been born in such a beautiful spot,' he said.

'Yes, it is beautiful,' I agreed. It was a lie, but this wasn't the time to say that for the poor, the moors and the mill towns were a miserable place to be born and die.

'Well, what brings you to see me?' he enquired.

I told Petersen about my relationship with Friede and how we had been dating since 1945. I explained to him that his mandatory work edict had landed her in an unspeakably horrible factory.

He interrupted my story and asked for the name of the company and its address, which he wrote down in a notebook on his desk. Petersen told me: 'The work programme has been very successful, it has helped businesses rebuild and assisted Hamburg in getting back on her feet. You have seen the suffering in the city; there is no other way to rebuild our country and transform our nation into a democratic state, but through sacrifice and hard work.'

'This is not in dispute,' I said, 'and it is not my business to find fault with your government. I am asking that you release my girlfriend from a dodgy operation that is only benefiting a corrupt factory owner.'

'So, what will she do to eat if she is released from this work order?'

Confidently, I said: 'I'm going to marry her.'

Petersen retorted: 'You know that is not possible at the moment.'

Smiling, I told him: 'You are probably more aware than me, but that law is being changed.'

179

The mayor nodded and I continued: 'I give you my word as an Englishman that I will provide for this woman and her family from this time forward. For this city to arise from the ashes, it needs not only capital and brawn, it needs hope. It needs people to trust each other again. I love this woman and she loves me. The burden is mine and mine alone,' I concluded, without understanding the gravity of my pledge.

Petersen tapped his finger on his desk for several moments. He asked me to stand outside his office while he concluded some business.

I went out to stand in the company of the statues. After twenty minutes, the Burgermeister opened his door and asked me to step inside and return to my seat.

'Herr Smith, I think you are a good man if somewhat idealistic. What you have said to me might be true, but most would ask the question: What is the cost for love and devotion in this new world? I don't know if you will be able to afford the price of your dedication to this romanticism. I hope you can, and I will throw a penny into your hat to aid your cause. I have ordered your girlfriend to be released today from her work at that factory. She will face no penalties. However,' he said sternly, 'she is now your responsibility. I trust I have made the right decision.'

'Yes, you have,' I said, thanking him profoundly. As I left, I turned to the mayor and asked him about the factory and the other women working there.

Petersen interrupted me. 'That is a different matter altogether. I make no promises, but I will see if they can be helped. Good day and good luck, Herr Smith.'

CHAPTER 18

Closing the ring

On 31 July 1946, the House of Lords struck down the marriage ban between British servicemen and ex-enemy nationals. I don't know if it was by design or omission, but the government didn't go out of its way to trumpet the right of servicemen to marry nationals from former belligerent countries. In fact, the news didn't reach me until mid-August, when I read an old copy of the *Daily Mail*. The announcement, momentous to me, was buried in its back pages between advertisements for hair tonic and football scores. The newspaper report made it official: I was free to marry Friede. Perhaps my life was to end on a happier note than predicted in dismal West Yorkshire.

I didn't rush out to buy Friede an engagement ring or confess to her this wonderful change of events. I was mindful that my enthusiasm was easily crushed by Friede's pragmatism. It was better to wait for a moment when we were alone and thoughtful. It was several days after I had read the news that I suggested we go to the Malcolm Club.

There we sat and drank wine on their outdoor deck into the late afternoon. It was a humid and lazy day and the sun danced through the leaves of the trees surrounding the club. Swans and ducks floated leisurely on the artificial lake. So that we could be alone, I invited her to go out on the water in a canoe with me.

There was no better place, I thought, to bring her the news that we were free to marry than on these calm and cool, flat waters during a hot summer's afternoon. I navigated us from the shore that rippled with laughter from couples enjoying a drink on the club's patio. Friede reclined at the bow, her right hand skimming the top of the water. She was half-asleep from the wine we had drunk.

'Luv,' I asked, 'where are you?'

Friede smiled and said, 'Here, as always, with you in a canoe. I will always be with you in this canoe at three o'clock in the summer time and the wine shall always be crisp and cool to my mouth.'

'We can be together like this for ever,' I told her.

She giggled: 'Your arms would get tired if you had to paddle for an eternity.' Friede's head was tilted towards the water. 'For ever for us must be the stray bits of time we are allowed to spend with each other. It can be nothing more than that.'

'No, I mean it,' I said. 'I have wonderful news; the government has lifted its ban on marriage to Germans. We can get married.'

Friede raised her hand from the water and dropped it back into the lake. She scooped water with the cup of her hand and splashed me until liquid beads ran down my shirt.

'Really?' she asked incredulously. 'So are you proposing?'

I laughed and said, 'Naturally, as I have wanted to since the day we met. Will you marry me, Elfriede Gisela Edelmann, and be my wife until we set like the sun?'

She scrambled over to my side of the canoe and almost tipped us into the lake. At first, she didn't say yes or no.

Instead, Friede kissed me and replied, 'We have much to discuss.'

What was there to discuss, I wondered. Marriage for my kind was simple – a trip to the registry office, a lunch at the pub, and the following morning back to the pits or the mills to punch the clock until retirement.

'You need to find out what we must do to get married. It may not be as simple as you think,' she said suspiciously.

'But you will marry me?' I asked.

Friede touched my face with her hand and answered, 'First, let's find out if it can be done. After that, you can take me in your canoe until the sun sets on our lives.'

So I did as Friede requested and spoke with my group captain to make sure we weren't tumbling into an ocean of regret.

My dealings with Group Captain Cox before my request for marriage were few, but he was agreeable to me marrying a German. 'You'll be the first under my command who has taken the plunge,' he said. 'However, it is not as simple as a marriage back in your home country.'

He told me it was going to take as long as a year to get the necessary permission to marry from the RAF and the British government. The group captain asked me to return in a week so he could gather the paperwork required to proceed with my request.

I wasn't put off by the seemingly endless time it would take to arrange my marriage to Friede. Actually, I welcomed it and hoped it was going to give me enough opportunity to get used to my new responsibilities. I had no happy examples from my life in Britain on how one succeeded in marriage. My only navigational guides were books, the cinema, and my instincts to not repeat the sins of my parents and surrender to poverty and hopelessness. The following week, I returned to the group captain's office. He handed me a series of forms and requisitions.

Looking serious, he said: 'The onus is on your fiancée to be like Caesar's wife, above reproach.'

It was explained to me that Friede had to first undergo some very intimate medical tests to determine if she was pregnant, suffering from any venereal diseases, or just medically unsound for Britain. If she passed the medical exams, the police were to examine her for political or criminal activity that would invalidate her for marriage to a British subject.

Cox took out a cigarette, lit it, and told me. 'As this is the first foreign national marriage under my command, don't cock it up for me or the squadron. Any sign of trouble, please abort your mission because all prying eyes from HQ are watching you, me, and this air base.'

After I was dismissed, I went straight to the cook in charge of the officers' mess hall. I wanted to get an extravagant wine, usually reserved for the officers' club, to celebrate my new status.

He wiped his hands on his greasy apron and declared: 'I got just the thing for two love birds who want to celebrate.' He went to the locked wine cabinet and produced two bottles of Bollinger 1938 champagne.

'How much is it?' I asked.

'It's a fiver for you because I've got a soft heart for love.'

I thanked him and tucked them away in my haversack. I

left the camp and went to meet Friede on Hamburg's high street, Jungfernstieg. It was several blocks north of the train station, and the expansive boulevard overlooked a small reservoir flowing in from the Alster River. The lake was filled with tiny sailboats navigating around a baroque water fountain positioned in the middle of the reservoir.

The war had not destroyed the street; its shops and restaurants were still intact. They did a bustling business with the families of old wealth and the nouveau riche. Jungfernstieg was inoculated against ration-book sadness and the despair of rootless refugees because the shoppers on this street knew their happiness was assured and as predictable as the fresh cream on their Sachertorte. They were the ones whose wealth and cynicism protected them while under fascism and now under occupation.

Friede and I had arranged to meet on a bench by the water. There, I explained my meeting with the group captain and the paper journey we would have to take to get married.

Friede shrugged her shoulders and calmly said, 'So be it. Now don't you think it is time you bought me an engagement ring?'

'I couldn't agree more,' I replied.

'I want something nice and simple, nothing extravagant,' she said as we left the bench to walk to a jewellery store.

I wondered why we couldn't get the ring on the black market. Friede, however, was adamant that buying an engagement ring from the black market would invite bad luck to our forthcoming marriage.

'We can't profit on the misery of others and hope to

live happily ever after. Simple is better,' she said, 'especially when it doesn't come wrapped around with someone else's sorrow.'

When we were in the jewellery store, Friede allowed me to act as if I knew what I was doing. I looked through the glass counter that held all types of diamond rings. I ran my finger down the case, like a boy trying to choose a treat from a sweetshop.

Finally, she cleared her throat and said, 'What do you think about that one?'

She pointed to a ring tucked away to the side. The saleswoman let me hold it. I looked at it with the keen eye of a 23 year-old unaccustomed to jewellery, to rings, and to testaments of everlasting love. Simplicity was its virtue. It was a simple band of gold, with five diamond chips studded around it. It didn't trumpet wealth, glamour or bad manners; it made a simple statement: beauty need only be devotion and trust in good or bad times.

Hesitantly, I asked: 'Is that what you would like?'

Friede nodded approvingly. She hastily left the store so I could purchase the ring.

Outside, she grabbed my arm and said, 'Take me to the botanical park. You can put the ring on my finger there.'

So beneath a row of beech trees, I knelt and asked her to marry me. When she said yes, I slipped the engagement ring on her finger. She kissed me and said excitedly, 'Now let's go tell Mutti.'

It was late when we arrived at her mother's apartment and Maria Edelmann was cleaning up the dishes from her evening meal. 'Tardy once more for dinner,' she noted in a

half-hearted tone of disapproval. 'You didn't miss much,' she
added with a sigh. 'It was potato soup again.'

When Friede waved her hand under her mother's nose
and displayed the ring, Maria's stern manner disappeared.
She embraced her daughter and kissed her affectionately.

'So you are to be married. This is a wonderful and happy
end after we have suffered so much through the war and
through the peace,' she exclaimed.

I produced the Bollinger and Friede's mother looked
over the bottle of pre-war French champagne. 'At least in
this life there is the pleasure of good champagne, a beautiful
daughter, and a new son-in-law to take away all of its hurt
and anguish.'

'Open it quickly,' Friede instructed me while Maria
fetched the Gellersons. I popped the cork and poured the
contents into some champagne flutes. We stood in the
kitchen and were toasted by her mother. 'To your new life –
may it be long, happy, and filled with riches and adventure.'

After a while, the Gellersons brought out their phonograph and everyone danced a circumscribed waltz with
Friede. When it came to my turn, Friede led and my feet
somehow moved with dignity and élan. Outside the apartment, the light dimmed as the late summer's darkness
slowly crept over the town.

CHAPTER 19

The RAF's prenuptial
poke and prod

When September came, the summer retreated behind dark, corpulent skies. Most days were overcast or foggy with pockets of rain. On many nights, water spattered against my bedroom window and thunder barked from low-hanging clouds. Across town during those evenings, Friede kept her mother awake until the early morning hours. Every aspect, detail and outcome of our wedding ceremony and reception was plotted by Friede and her mother.

Friede believed our union was going to put an end to any questions about her and her mother's illegitimate start in this world. She wanted our marriage to extinguish the stigma of being a bastard. Finally, all the shame and humiliation Friede had endured as a child and teenager would vanish by the marriage registrar's signature.

Maria Edelmann cautioned her daughter that the walk to the altar was a long road. It was best to be mindful of the dangers that lay ahead. Friede's mother was a keen observer and victim of life's cruelties, punishments and trials of patience. Maria knew that unhappiness was often a visitor who called on those who demanded a different destiny than they were allotted at birth.

Friede dismissed her mother's prescience to me as

widow's envy. 'Mutti is just nervous for me because men were happy to share her bed but never her life.'

It was mid-September when the group captain's adjutant, Flight Lieutenant Locke, informed me that Friede's medical examination was to take place at Wandsbek hospital in Hamburg.

I asked her if she would be all right going alone. Friede laughed and asked, 'What can they possibly do to me? German doctors have examined me before without any problems.'

Unfortunately, Friede had never experienced the cold hands of a disgruntled British army doctor. From the moment she entered the hospital, Friede was treated like livestock with possible foot and mouth infection. Her reception wasn't surprising, considering the hospital wing was designated for British personnel; a German who was neither a cleaner nor a cook in that section of the hospital was regarded as something close to a contagion.

The admitting nurse, fearing that her comprehension of English was insufficient, yelled instructions at Friede, following a simple rule that our island had employed for centuries: English was best digested by foreigners in a blustering tone.

Friede was rewarded with less dignity and more intrusiveness than a new recruit would receive during an RAF medical inspection. They took her to a cold room in the hospital's basement, where she was interrogated by an obese GP from Putney. He noted on Friede's medical files her age, her hair and eye colour, that she had all her teeth. In between chain-smoking cigarettes, the doctor asked about

her family's medical history. Were there any idiots or enfee-
bled relatives, any genetic defects from madness to mental
retardation in her background?

Friede answered his questions with a polite yes or no.
She wanted no shade of doubt to colour his assessment. The
doctor continued his questions and discovered that Friede
was illegitimate. He told her that it was his opinion that
Germany was a country loose in morals.

After the oral interview was complete, the fat GP from
Putney ordered Friede to disrobe. A matron who must have
learned her nursing skills in Broadmoor prison assisted
him in the examination. Friede was probed like she was the
Elephant Man.

She was palpated, weighed and measured while the
doctor coughed phlegmily. Blood samples were taken, followed by urine and stool samples. Friede was X-rayed and
inspected for TB. Her day ended with a painful and humili-
ating rough inspection of her sexual organs. During the
gynaecological examination, the overweight doctor quizzed
Friede about her sexual encounters. He asked her when she
became sexually active. He asked her how many sexual partners she had had in her life. Mortified, she told the doctor
that it was irrelevant as it was evident that she was healthy
and free of any disease.

The GP insisted on the necessity of compliance. It was
impossible otherwise for him to complete the examination
or for her to be allowed to marry. Defeated, she answered
each question in a monotone voice and her responses were
written down by the assisting matron.

When the ordeal was over, Friede related to me that she

didn't know what the doctor disliked most: women, sex, or just Germans.

Friede told me that when the medical inquisition ended, the physician bestowed upon her one last insult. He bade her goodbye while he lit a cigarette from the dying embers of his last one and said, 'Not for me to say, but I think it is just bloody wrong for you to be allowed to marry one of our kind. Your lot are nothing but bloody Nazis. Good day, madam.'

Friede left the hospital and returned home where she cried in her mother's arms, declaring 'It was just horrible, unspeakable, and barbaric.'

The results from her medical examination were sent to RAF HQ Germany, where they remained for weeks. Finally, a clerk dispatched them by sea to a nondescript office in London. There, an unknown cipher would decide whether Friede was chaste and healthy enough to marry the son of a coal miner.

While we waited nervously for the results of Friede's examination, the first stage of the Nuremberg war crime trials concluded. The outcome wasn't surprising, considering the overwhelming evidence against the accused. The Nazi architects who orchestrated the war, the Holocaust and the systematic looting of the occupied countries were found guilty. Out of the 21 defendants in history's first trial for crimes against humanity, eleven were condemned to death.

Hang them quickly, I thought, it's time to get on with it and be done with this evil past. Around camp, there was little talk about a former foreign minister and some field marshals who sat uncomfortably in their cells awaiting the hangman's call. It was beyond our rank or our comprehension of evil to offer any opinion other than: "'anging's too good fer 'em. Drop those dirty Nazi bastards into the sea from a Lanc and let 'em sink.'

As for me, I spent no great energy reflecting on their guilt or their specious claims that they were just following orders. I was more apprehensive about Friede's medical reports. I wanted the results as quickly as possible so we might proceed with our wedding plans. As the condemned in Nuremberg no doubt wished to slow down time, Friede and I wanted it to fly furiously towards our future together. Time, however, passed as it should, one second after the other, one hour after the other, until each man or woman's fate was revealed.

I thought perhaps we might have some positive news before Friede's birthday, but nothing arrived from London. It was probably foolish to believe that her medical report was going to be processed during that week. It was too soon and we were mere granules of sand in the Royal Air Force's order of commitments.

The military might have been sluggish in analysing Friede's medical examination; however, on setting an execution date for Nuremberg's eleven condemned men, they were expeditious. The men were to swing on 16 October. Hermann Göring, former head of the Luftwaffe and morphine addict, cheated justice the day before his scheduled appointment with God. A sympathetic guard smuggled in a cyanide capsule, which Göring used to commit suicide. In Hamburg, the general consensus was good riddance, considering that Göring's incompetence had assisted the Allies in levelling their city.

We celebrated Friede's nineteenth birthday without any word back from London.

'Next year,' I said, 'you will be a married woman and we will never have to depend on the government again.'

Friede laughed and replied: 'We must wait and see about next year. Your government hasn't even said yet whether I am medically fit to marry an Englishman.'

With all this waiting, my patience began to fray and wear like a jacket worn for too many years through good and bad seasons. My daily visits to the adjutant officer's duty room were a disappointment.

'Sorry, perhaps tomorrow, you know the wheels of government. They turn as slow as a mill stone.'

Guy Fawkes Day rushed upon us and I saw the days shorten and the nights lengthen. November lumbered onwards, the cold winds from the Baltic returned, and snow and sleet fell onto the streets of Hamburg. Winter was upon us and I grew downhearted. The wait for Friede's medical clearance was endless and malicious for me. I was about to resign myself to another month of grinding anticipation when the adjutant officer informed me one morning at breakfast that Friede was healthy enough to marry a Brit.

'Now we will need a thorough police and background check to see if her soul is as clean as her lungs,' he told me with a laugh. He wished me good luck and added: 'Life would be a damn sight easier if we didn't have to contend with these fools in government, drowning us in paperwork.'

The following day, Friede went with me to the police station located on her mother's street. She requested they complete a criminal and political background check on her for the British government. We were lucky that it was the same duty sergeant who had investigated her grandfather's suicide.

He remembered me and said, 'It was in unhappier circumstances the last time we met.'

I handed him a few packs of cigarettes to show my appreciation. He said he would try his best to have the information back to the RAF within a month. The sergeant realistically pointed out to us the problems in obtaining any documents from before or during the war. 'It is difficult, you know, because most of the records in Hamburg were destroyed in the bombing.'

So during that December month, someone from what remained of Hamburg's civil service climbed through stacks of documents to collect Friede's political and security history.

It was time, I decided, to let my sister and my mother know that I was going to marry Friede in 1947. I wrote my sister a Christmas card: 'I am happy. Wish me luck and let's hope I don't bugger it up.' I also enclosed some money and a snap of Friede and me.

I was more apprehensive about informing my mother Lillian. I would have preferred to not tell her until the last moment, fearing her bitter tongue. In her return letter, my mother didn't acknowledge my announcement, but did ask for money: 'For keeping body and soul alive,' as she put it.

My sister wrote back to congratulate me: 'Mam being Mam called you a daft bugger when she learned about your upcoming marriage. She'll be a right cow until the holy ghost takes her kicking and screaming out of this world. It's smashing news,' Mary wrote. 'I can't wait to see you back home where you were born and bred with your woman beside you.'

I loved my sister and knew that her devotion to me was absolute. Yet her words about my birthplace, my so-called homeland of Halifax, Bradford and West Yorkshire, made me cringe and squirm like a ferret in a cage. It was a terrible place, as odious and cruel for me as the cracked concrete floor where butchers let the blood of pigs drip clean. I planned to stay in Germany in the RAF for as long as possible because I was sure that Friede couldn't survive the harshness of life in Halifax.

CHAPTER 20

Bizonia as usual

In December 1946, a prehistoric deep freeze smothered Europe; and like a glacier, the cold stretched deep into the New Year. Eighteen months after the surrender, life in the occupied city was still nasty, brutish, and short. During that winter, Hamburg was the literal spot where hell froze over for anyone down on his luck. Resentment towards the British occupation forces grew among the inhabitants as the thermometer plummeted to inhospitable temperatures. People grumbled vigorously about every indignity and shortage they endured, from inadequate food rations to insignificant coal allotments to heat their stoves.

The population was impatient. They wanted their standard of existence to change from this porridge-bowl reality that they believed was foisted on them as retribution for the war. Germans pointed their fingers towards their overlords: the British and the Americans. They were to blame, they whispered, for their hunger, their cold, and their destitution. The occupation leaders realised that the docile and pliant German population was going to turn into an angry mob if not placated.

A consensus developed among the Western occupying governments that, outside of biblical revenge, governing Germany as a series of medieval states served no purpose. Punitively denying the German people anything but a pre-twentieth-century existence wasn't only costly – if the strategy were to continue, it would breed a hostile population with a tepid allegiance to both Britain and America. However, returning occupied Germany to its industrialised, no-nonsense capitalistic society was a difficult, if not impossible, undertaking for the Allies. The Western sectors were subdivided into occupation zones controlled by Britain, the USA, and, to a much lesser degree, France. Each country ran their segment as judiciously as possible but to the benefit of their mother country. Growth was stifled through tariffs, trade barriers and a prohibition on the free flow of labour between occupation zones.

America and Britain begrudgingly accepted that reducing Germany to an agrarian society benefited no one, except perhaps Russia. However, by 1946, the Soviet Union was considered a dodgy ally at best and a possible belligerent at worst. Many political operatives began to accept that Russia was perhaps as dangerous and as aggressive as Nazi Germany was in the 1930s.

London and Washington gradually sobered to the fact that the Soviets had not liberated Eastern Europe at the cost of twenty million soldiers to germinate democracy. It was to create an empire as diabolical and cruel as Hitler's policy of Lebensraum.

The United States and Great Britain agreed that their occupation sectors were to be gradually transformed from a defeated vassal state into a new German nation. The new country could act as a buffer against any future Russian aggression. The genesis of this new state was an economic union between the British and American spheres of influence. This new trade zone was to be called Bizonia. It was a name assured to set no German heart aflutter with nationalistic pride, unless of course he was an accountant, businessman or enterprising spiv.

For the worker picking through the rubble in British-controlled Hamburg, American-controlled Frankfurt or the hundred or so other gutted Stadts and Burgs, this new economic union did little to improve their day-to-day existence. However, for the businessman or the black marketeer attempting to turn an honest or dishonest dollar into an immense profit, it was a new and bright beginning.

While economists and bankers hailed the creation of Bizonia as a giant leap towards Europe's future, I was more interested in getting my own house in order. I was almost 24 and impatient to marry Friede. I was finding the paperwork and the multi-layered sets of approvals we needed for our wedding more insurmountable by the day. It was only natural that my love life and my own future occupied my imagination more than resuscitating the German wolf to keep Russia on guard in her new and enlarged lair. The men with briefcases and dark sunglasses were free to do their deals with old Nazi capitalists. It was none of my business as long as I was left alone to get on with the least amount of interference. Yet while questionable Nazi industrialists lined up to rebuild their commercial empires without impediments, Friede's own politics were scrutinised.

At the same moment Bizonia was born at the end of January 1947, I was called into a meeting with the adjutant officer about Friede's security clearance. When I arrived at his office, Flight Lieutenant Locke looked as apprehensive as a bank manager upon review of a shaky business overdraft.

'There were issues of concern,' the flight lieutenant announced.

'What concerns?' I asked incredulously.

He cleared his throat. 'You know Elfriede Edelmann's mother was a Nazi.'

Not this again, I thought.

Politely, I tried to explain Maria Edelmann's reasons. 'Yes, she joined the Nazi party, but she was hardly friends with the Bormanns,' I replied sarcastically. 'My understanding is that Maria Edelmann's involvement with the Nazi party was limited to paying its yearly dues. Maria joined the party late in the war. That hardly indicates a dyed-in-the-wool Nazi. Look,' I continued, 'this woman was pressured to join the party.'

'How so?' asked the officer.

'She was engaged in a love affair with a married man who was a former politician and a notable businessman named Karp. He gave no truck to the Nazis, but he did trade with them. I think you should also know that Maria Edelmann was under considerable pressure to join the party because Friede, my wife-to-be, is illegitimate. Moreover, her father was a socialist and communist sympathiser.'

'I wasn't aware of this,' said the adjutant. 'And what are your fiancée's current politics?'

I replied: 'The same as mine. We want to live in a society where we are free; we can work for a fair wage and live in a decent home. We don't go much in for politics, except to know you can't trust them after they've got your vote.'

He thought for a while and announced: 'This is really absurd; I will write to HQ and explain that there is nothing to this news about her mother. While we are awaiting their response, I'd advise you to get a letter from the civilian authorities that will attest to her good character. When are you planning to marry?' he asked.

'We were thinking about the late summer.'

'We should be able to give you the go ahead to marry well before then.'

'I hope so,' I said and left his office.

When Friede asked about the security check, I lied and said, 'No problems, it's been approved. We'd better start working on getting you that letter attesting to your good character.'

'That will not be a problem,' she responded. 'Mutti has already arranged a letter from one of Uncle Henry's associates who knows the new mayor.'

'So, your mother is still in contact with her dead lover's connections?' I asked.

'Of course,' she replied, 'and why not? Mutti was like a wife to Henry. No one from his business thinks ill of her.' Friede then grabbed me by the arm and sat me down at the kitchen table. She told me: 'What we really must talk about is our wedding day.'

It was something I hadn't given much thought to up until that moment. The same couldn't be said of Friede, who had given much consideration to the details surrounding her wedding day. The notion of marriage, legitimacy, and a union recognised by society had occupied her daydreams from the time she was a lonely child.

It was a simple motif that kept her strong as a little girl. It was the belief that her mother and she were going to be rescued by a prince. As a forlorn and lost child, this fantasy gave Friede great comfort. It was a source of consolation and an emotional retreat from the two worlds Friede straddled: the weekday plebeian life in the care of her foster parents and the bohemian existence she experienced with her mother on weekends.

At around the age of seven, Friede dreamed that her real father Fritz would return from Berlin and marry her mother in a fairytale wedding. It was a make-believe world drawn by an imaginative child who wanted to be envied by the other schoolgirls rather than be the object of their teasing. As Friede grew older, the daydream matured and she realised that Fritz wasn't coming back to marry her mother and legitimise his daughter. So, as a teenager it was her hope that Henry Karp, her mother's lover, would make an honest woman of her mother. It became a teenage obsession that Henry would marry her mother and adopt her as his daughter. When Henry died of a heart attack in 1944, Friede accepted that her mother was condemned by society to be the fallen woman. Friede, however, was never going to concede to the same fate.

To Friede, marriage was more than just a contract of love between two young adults. Our ceremony was to be the instrument that corrected the mistakes of her family's history and her illegitimacy. It was necessary that our wedding day captured and replicated the intricate map she had drawn and redrawn since childhood. Our wedding was to bring to fruition her dream of stability, respectability, and honour.

Over a few glasses of wine, Friede unfolded her vision of our wedding. She insisted that the wedding was to be intimate, neither too big nor too small. It must be a great celebration for everybody who attended it.

'It will be something,' she said, 'our friends and family will remember for a lifetime. Will your family come from Britain?'

I replied without a hint of sarcasm. 'I don't think they will be coming. They have never left the north and I don't think my wedding or funeral would budge them. They would only go if it was in Blackpool and we paid for the dodgem ride afterwards.'

Friede was intrigued to know what weddings were like back in Britain. I explained to her the only time I witnessed a wedding was as a delivery boy bringing the victuals for the feast. In my class, I told her most weddings were civil ceremonies with a ploughman's lunch reception to follow.

'What about your parents' wedding?'

I laughed. 'It would be safe to say that no one in my Dad's family and no one in my Mam's family were happy that day. If there were any tears shed, they were of regret.'

Friede looked cross with me. I tried to placate her by telling her that our wedding was going to come as close to her dreams as humanly possible.

Friede's wedding plans weren't ostentatious or pretentious, but they were comprehensive. It was imperative that our wedding service be conducted in a church. The announcement took me by surprise and made me almost cough out the drink I had just swallowed. Up until her declaration, I really hadn't considered the church of my youth, her church, or anyone else's church as ever again being involved in my life. A miserable childhood spent in the guilt-ridden and brutal hands of semi-sober nuns and priests had left me distrustful of any institution that promised salvation while beating my backside blue.

I couldn't remember the last time I had been in a church, let alone been to confession and taken communion. It certainly didn't appeal to me, returning to church and having a priest absolve me of my crimes against God. I wasn't even sure if Friede understood the gravity of what she requested from me. So I tried to gently persuade her against a religious ceremony.

'You know I am a Roman Catholic,' I told her, with about as much pleasure as if I were admitting to membership of the Nazi party. 'It's not that I hold much love for Rome,' I continued, 'but I think it might be a problem to marry in another faith because who knows how long conversion takes?'

'Of course, I know. I don't mind becoming a Catholic,' she responded. 'I think they might be better Christians than the Lutherans, who are all so mortified by guilt. Remember what I told you at the Michel church so long ago: it is not necessarily God that I believe in, but some spirit of creation, some energy that is beyond our comprehension.'

I kept quiet and tried to respect Friede's spiritual acceptance of things I believed to be rot. God, I believed, and his acolytes had caused a lot of bother and destruction in my life and the lives of millions of other poor supplicants. However, at this moment I wasn't going to let him get in the way of my happiness with Friede.

So I postponed any more talk about Catholicism. 'Let's work on the conversion at a later time,' I told her.

I changed the subject to what I considered an easier problem to solve. 'What about your wedding dress?'

Little did I realise that to obtain a wedding dress in 1947 Germany was as arduous as going on a crusade for the Holy Grail.

Friede looked at me and responded seriously. 'A wedding dress cannot be bought; it must be unique and one of a kind. It must be created from a beautiful fabric by an expert dressmaker.'

Talking about her wedding dress made me realise I was swimming in the deep end without a lifejacket. So I stopped speaking, smiled, and waited to see if Friede had a solution to her wedding gown. It didn't take her long to assure me that she knew the right people to deal with this delicate situation.

'We have no problems; I already have a dressmaker. Frau Schröder, she is an old friend of my mother's. Before the British came, she was the number one dressmaker for an excellent shop in Hamburg. We can go and see her tomorrow. Frau Schröder will sort everything out for us,' Friede explained with a satisfied voice.

I exhaled and told her, 'Well, that's a relief. It seems you have most things covered.'

'Yes, she has already measured me.'

It felt odd to have all of this secret activity occurring under my nose. At one moment, I was relieved that many matters relating to this wedding were being handled by others. At other moments, it was as if my intention to be married was being hijacked by someone else's convention. I began to worry about the cost of the wedding and whether I was leaving myself and Friede open for disappointment. I kept quiet about my doubts because it was impossible to derail Friede's excitement over her wedding. I didn't want to dampen her belief that this ceremony would transform her from a disjointed, passionate nineteen-year-old girl into a serious-minded woman.

Our nuptials were like an ancient rite of passage to her. I didn't know what they were to me except a means to keep my love from flying away and an attempt to put down roots that my own parents were denied by bad luck.

I realised that if I thought too much about the mechanics of the actual wedding day, I'd go into a funk and begin to doubt the worth of it. I resolved to accept her wishes passively and hoped that the day and our future weren't going to be a disappointment for either of us.

'Tomorrow, Frau Schröder is going to show me her preliminary designs. You must bring her some coffee so she knows we can pay for her services.'

On the following afternoon, we travelled to Frau Schröder's house. The woman lived with her husband in a comfortable bungalow located near the Alster. Her husband greeted us at the door. He was military-thin and had a shock of white hair running down his forehead. He looked arrogant and baronial to me, but he greeted Friede warmly. I received a stiff handshake and an aloof hello. No one ever told me what he did in the war and I never asked, but I was sure that whatever it was, he was a devotee of Hitler.

Frau Schröder was a thin, prim and exacting woman

who was several years older than Friede's mother. She appreciated my gesture of a half kilo of coffee and thanked me graciously. Her words were amiable, but across her face there was an implied expression: I was a fool if I thought the dress she was making was an inconsequential undertaking.

At the start of our meeting, Friede and I sat with the elderly couple in their parlour, which was furnished in oppressive heavy furniture. After a few minutes, Frau Schröder left the room and returned with a sketchbook.

She looked at me caustically and announced, 'It would be bad luck for you to see the dress before your wedding day. Please talk with Herr Schröder while I show Friede these drawings.'

I got up from the heavy sofa and moved to sit near her husband, who didn't look pleased at my arrival. He exchanged a curt and dismissive smile and tried to ignore me.

Across the parlour, Friede and Frau Schröder flipped through her sketchbook. The dressmaker made notes while Friede whispered ideas in her ear. The conspiratorial way the two women viewed the sketches of the wedding dress, one might have thought they were approving the blueprints for the *Bismarck*. After a while, they finished their deliberations and the sketchbook was closed shut with satisfaction.

Coffee and cake were served. Frau Schröder presented an elegant cake, triple-layered in what appeared to be butter cream. As I tried to enjoy my cake and coffee, Frau Schröder spoke to me about the dress.

'You know this is a one-of-a-kind dress.'

I smiled ignorantly and said, 'But of course.'

The old dressmaker looked at me impatiently. Friede interrupted and explained: 'What Frau Schröder means is my dress will be made from silk, and silk is impossible to come by in Hamburg. It is also very expensive.'

My heart dropped a beat. 'Can we make the dress from another fabric?'

'Of course not,' shouted Frau Schröder.

'What are we to do then?'

'It has been taken care of,' Friede said. 'We have the material, but it is unfortunately in Brussels. It is a wedding gift from Uncle Henry's partner, Herr Rodmann. However, he cannot get a travel permit to go there, so perhaps you can go to Brussels to pick up the material.'

'That is very considerate of Uncle Henry's partner,' I responded.

Friede smiled and added: 'He was pleased to do something for us. It was the least he could do considering how Henry helped conceal his communist past from the Nazis.'

Frau Schröder interrupted to insist that I make the trip as soon as possible so that she could get to work on the dress. 'I don't want any problems,' she said, 'with the material.'

I told the women I would get a pass to travel to Belgium as soon as possible. When I walked Friede back home from the Schröders', her footsteps were light and she beamed with happiness. I said to her: 'You'd better give me all of the instructions to get the dress materials.'

Friede stopped and spoke with some hesitation. 'There is one other thing; it is nothing, but Uncle Henry's partner has asked that you take a letter with you to Belgium. He wants you to give the letter to the person who has our silk for the dress.'

'What is the letter about?' I asked suspiciously.

'It is nothing for us to be concerned with. He just wants to resume contact with old business partners. You know what everyone is saying now: it is business as usual.'

CHAPTER 21

Grand Place, Brussels

A month after Frau Schröder commanded me to go to Belgium, I was granted leave to travel to Brussels. It was fortuitous that my travel warrant was delayed because I needed to save extra money for the trip. The moment Friede's mother learned about my journey, she suggested it was wise to also purchase lace for Friede's veil.

'If you are going to travel that far for her dress material, it would be foolish not to buy Belgian lace, as it is the world's finest,' Maria told me knowledgeably. 'Perhaps,' Friede added, 'while you are there, you can look for some wedding shoes for me.'

Dutifully, I nodded my head and said that was an excellent idea. The growing extravagance of our nuptials worried me. My RAF wireless pay wasn't much and I was living life like an officer with an annuity. I wasn't in debt, but I was running a tight line between solvency and destitution. Were it not for the perks of living overseas in a country where everyone was on the fiddle, my romantic life would have been more circumspect and certainly less eventful. Anxious as I was about covering the outlay, I still wanted to create a perfect wedding day for Friede and for myself.

I dreaded that my wish to please and be pleased in return was setting both Friede and me up for future disappointments. Nobody I was acquainted with had had a white wedding, with a church service and an afternoon reception along with numerous pre-marriage parties. I was frightened my life was going pear-shaped and it was going to be witnessed by everyone I knew as if it were up on the cinema screen.

I even complained to Sid about my misgivings. Fortunately, he was wise enough to know that it was better to have a go rather than sit the dance out.

'How many times are you going to get married, mate? Sure, it's over the top if you were back at home, but you're not. Live it up because there won't be much when you're back in Britain with the missus except fond memories to go with your mushy peas and chips.'

'Right you are,' I said.

No matter the price and damn the consequences, I was going to marry Friede in style. I'd pay the piper and go to Brussels to get Friede's material for her wedding dress.

My travel warrant to Belgium was only valid for 24 hours, so I booked passage on a locomotive that left the Bahnhof at six in the morning. To keep me warm and fed on the way, the camp cook packed me a lunch with a thermos generously filled with whisky and coffee. Dave drove me to the station. He promised to return at midnight when my train was due to arrive back in the city.

I found a window seat on the train and watched Hamburg disappear into a whirl of steam and snow. I felt at peace with myself because this wrecked maritime metropolis had beguiled and seduced me. Hamburg's independent come-as-you-are attitude made me feel like I belonged with its diverse citizens. I closed my eyes and listened to the rhythm of the train as it sped along the track and I travelled further away from the city.

For the first time in my life, I was sure that regardless of the distance covered that day, there was someone who loved me and was waiting for me in Hamburg.

My train companions were mostly British soldiers being shunted to other occupation areas. On board there were also a few British civilian government workers. They were easy to recognise by their wool overcoats, thin lips, and cynical expressions. During the long trip, they were as supercilious as public schoolboys who thought they were destined for better things than riding an uncomfortable train through the wreckage of Germany's heartland.

It was still well below freezing that day and, at times, the scenery disappeared into a blinding snowstorm. In spite of the nasty weather, labourers were outside in the cold rebuilding ruined structures or driving horse-drawn carts filled with rubble, coal or firewood. At each train stop, the engine snorted like a beast recovering from a gallop. Sometimes, I wiped the window clean of condensation with the palm of my hand and peered onto the soot-stained railway station's platform. Standing on it, there was a familiar cast of characters: hustlers, lost refugees, and orphaned children harvesting cigarette butts. Nobody else in my compartment seemed to notice or care about these flash photographs of desperate folk. Some of the soldiers played cards while the civilians in suits talked in clipped accents about forthcoming summer vacations in France.

After many hours staring out of the joyless window, we finally reached Cologne, which meant we were near the border. It also indicated that we had crossed over into the American sector. GIs began to swagger on board. Their cocky self-assuredness turned the civil servants' faces sour with envy and disgust, but I welcomed their independent optimism over our self-defeated aloofness.

As the train drew closer to its final destination, I grew excited about seeing Belgium. Just before the end of the war, my unit was briefly stationed at an abandoned Luftwaffe airfield on the outskirts of Antwerp. The few short weeks I spent there were my first experience in a different country with a diverse culture. I enjoyed Belgium in the winter of 1945, despite battles raging only a hundred kilometres away from me. I wondered how the country had changed from those final days of conflict, when it was used as a marshalling yard, pushing troops up into Holland or across the Siegfried Line.

The border control at the frontier was minimal. A jolly, rotund Belgian customs guard made a cursory check of my travel papers. Looking outside, Belgium appeared well recovered from the war. Across the lowland countryside, the villages and hamlets seemed undamaged and prosperous. I saw giant cauldrons of smoke blazing from chimney pots on top of Flemish cottages. In the fields, fat milk cows exercised in pastures covered in a thin blanket of snow. Even the roadways were overweight with private and commercial vehicles belching black petrol fumes against the open skyline.

When the locomotive steamed through Brussels towards the station, it was a marvel to see a vibrant city, clean and free of bombing debris. The train arrived just after lunch hour at the city's Nord terminal. There were no wastrels and waifs blocking my exit on the train platform. Instead, it was filled with young Belgian women wearing the newest hairstyles. They were wrapped smartly in furs. Dazed, I bumped against them and excused myself. Their laughter, along with the smell of expensive perfume and carefree days, trailed after me. Those females at the station wore a prettiness that most German girls in Hamburg couldn't afford. Here, the girls had the luxury of being attractive without being hungry. It was revealing and wonderful to look at them enjoying being youthful, without a cynical and harsh world demanding that they pawn themselves for survival.

I walked from the station hall into a large thoroughfare. From my greatcoat pocket I pulled out my instructions from Friede. Her note told me to proceed to the Grand Place, Brussels' main square. When I arrived there I was astounded by its sheer beauty and that it was completely intact. There was no destruction, no burial pyres of bricks and mortar. It was a wonderful and revealing cityscape. Looking around at this unmolested capital, I realised for the first time that the war was over.

The parts of Brussels I walked through looked confidently towards their future. Living for so long in occupied Germany, I had grown used to the atmosphere of defeat and horrendous daily suffering. Hamburg made one think that the world was at the razor's edge, ready to be bled in sacrifice to a pagan god. Brussels was like fresh air in a room stifled by stale cigar smoke.

I regretted not having the time to explore more of Brussels, but my instructions were exact. It wasn't difficult to find the shop where I was supposed to exchange the letter from Uncle Henry's partner for the silk for Friede's wedding dress. It was a luxurious tobacco store located on a side street near a palace the RAF occupied and used as a hotel for military personnel on leave.

When I entered the store it was empty of customers. There was a man about my age arranging a pipe display. I walked over to him and smiled. I told him I had come from Hamburg with a letter for the owner. The clerk excused himself and walked into an office located at the rear of the store.

After several minutes the owner, a woman, appeared. She carried in her arms a package wrapped in brown paper. She asked my name. When I told her, she said, 'With my compliments,' and we exchanged our holdings.

Our swap took less than five minutes. Afterwards, the owner disappeared to the rear of the store and I exited. For the briefest of times, I wondered what might be in the letter, but was more than satisfied with what I had received in return.

I carefully stored the silk for the dress in my haversack and looked for a shoe shop. At the other end of the Grand Place I located a stylish store. There I provided a cut-out of Friede's feet and explained the purpose for the shoes. The saleswoman brought me an assortment of shoes, each more expensive than a year's wages for me. I explained in pigeon French that I was on a budget.

Displeased, the sales clerk found a beautiful pair of white shoes, but said, 'Sadly this is last year's style.'

'It will have to do,' I told her, 'because this year's money doesn't buy much in Brussels.'

After purchasing them, I asked the clerk if she could direct me to a lace shop to purchase material for the veil.

The salesgirl responded in a snotty accent, 'You will not be so lucky to find last year's style with lace; it hasn't changed in a hundred years.'

I was in Brussels for a little under five hours but I spent three months' wages. Walking back to the station, I felt satisfied that I had done well with my money. At the lace market, I was even able to buy my sister a delicately knitted handkerchief. By the time I got back to the station, I desperately wanted a beer or something to eat but the coins in my pocket rattled forlornly.

I walked around the station looking for a café. Instead, I spotted a fruit-monger's stall where bunches of ripe yellow bananas hung like exotic jewellery. Until that moment, the closest I had come to a banana was viewing them at the cinema on Carmen Miranda's head. They were as rare to me as pearls from the South China Sea.

I wondered what they tasted like, and I wasn't even sure if you ate the peel. I hurried over to the fruit stand and marvelled that the seller had more bananas hanging in his tiny stall than I thought the whole of the tropics could produce. I pulled the change out of my pockets and pointed at a ripe bunch. The monger took pity on me. He counted the money out of my hand and let me take twenty bananas.

On the journey home to Hamburg, there were no seats and I was forced to stand in the aisle. My bag filled with the silk and lace for Friede's dress was kept safe and guarded behind my legs. For the length of the trip, I held on to the banana bunch and only ate two of them. I was determined that the rest were to be a treat for Friede's family. The taste from the banana lingered with me from Liège until we arrived at the Bahnhof.

When Dave picked me up and noticed my fruit cargo, he asked, 'Where have you been now, the bloody Congo?'

CHAPTER 22

The Boothtown Road prodigal

In 1947, after the snow, the prehistoric low temperatures, the ice and the sleet, Europe was subjected to biblical winter rains. Torrential flooding occurred in Britain, Germany and many other parts of the Continent. Hamburg's gutters turned into rivers and its bomb craters into lakes filled with black, polluted water. It was rumoured that the sun had gone into exile from our hemisphere. We kept warm fires raging in our mess hut, but it still took a long time to burn the chill out of my bones. For the rest of Germany, they burned what they found – coal dust, wood chips and books – to keep hypothermia away. Back in Friede's apartment, her mother fed damp kindling into their wood stoves. It sparked, sizzled and fumed, releasing a foggy heat throughout their rooms.

It was miserable inside Germany and the situation wasn't much better for a lot of other countries. Hunger, corruption and violence lingered and poisoned much of western Europe. Greece succumbed to civil war. Italy teetered between anarchy and total decay. Great Britain was sinking in nature's downpour along with an insurmountable war debt. Across the Home Counties, housing was in short supply or inadequate for working families. Even with a socialist government, decent paying employment was hard to find. The empire that every schoolchild knew to

217

be Britain's right by God was dying. India, the jewel in the crown, battled for independence from us while the rest of our colonies waited restlessly for the end of their subjection.

On the Continent, western Europe asked what path we must follow: the capitalism of America or the collectivisation of Russia. No one really knew the answer or the outcome to that reply except that they wanted a decent life for themselves and their children. As the weather grew more and more inhospitable, voices from German citizens demanded to know when their yoke of occupation would end.

It was underneath those wet, black and unfriendly skies that the British government finally approved Friede's security clearance. We were free to marry. Some man in a damp suit with a name like Tastscome or Longnarrow placed his initials on her file and stamped it harmless to British interests. The gatekeepers eventually understood that Friede was nineteen and only endangered conformity. When it was agreed that her political background was risk-free, I was granted home leave. It was the last requirement before permission was granted to marry a former enemy national. The return home was supposed to be a cold splash of water for the serviceman intent on marrying a German girl. It was the government's logic that a trip home might remind the lad that there were pretty lasses down at his local who fancied him. The government's other motive was the hope that the serviceman's mother would knock some sense into him with a clout behind the ear.

My sense of hearth and home wasn't revived when I returned to Halifax and my mother's house. Riding the bus

from the station to Boothtown Road was like being elec-
trocuted with a cattle prod. As I sat smoking on the bus's
upper deck, all of the negative emotions from my youth in
this blighted northern county regurgitated into the back
of my throat. Everything in Halifax, from the people to
the buildings, looked in need of a good scrub. There was
two centuries of industrial muck on every brick facade and
on the blanched almond faces of my fellow bus riders. I
laughed to myself and thought that in Halifax the rains
were always plentiful, but they never washed the grime
away from this town.

The last time I had taken leave to see my family was in
1941. Nothing had changed on this street or any other road
in Halifax. Each one looked sad and neglected; the city was
a cul-de-sac to trap unhappiness.

When I walked up to the front stoop of my mother's
cramped tenement on Boothtown Road, there was no wel-
coming committee to greet me. The milkman, I thought
as I rattled the front door, would have received a warmer
welcome than me. The moment the door opened I knew
that she, like the town, the road, the houses, and the thankless lives most led in Halifax, was no different than when I
had left. Like everything else in Halifax, my Mam had just
become stouter.

My mother's looks had once been her source of pride
and comfort. In her youth and well into her middle age, my
mother's shapely body had turned the heads of miners, mill
workers and itinerant labourers. Years of drinking generous portions of lager had turned her into a fleshy tank of a
woman. The extra weight didn't make her look fat, it made

her seem like she was wearing body armour underneath her clothing.

Even though I had given sufficient forewarning of my arrival, the first words out of her mouth to me were, 'You'll have to make do with a cold spam butty. We got nowt extra because of the rationing.'

Time may wear down the rocks on Brighton beach, but it seemed to sharpen my Mam's anger at the world and the resentment she carried for her own brood. 'Never you mind, Mam,' I said. 'I ate well this morning and I'm in town only for a day and a night.'

'That's a pity,' my mother said with some doubt in her voice. 'Well, give us a kiss anyway.'

Afterwards, I followed her into the kitchen where I found Bill Moxon hovering near a steaming kettle. He was her lover, drinking companion, and sparring partner. Moxon had replaced my father in my mother's bed some twenty years earlier. I always had the suspicion that he regretted that fateful leg-over more than if he had killed a man and spent the succeeding years in jail.

Age or my mother's overpowering personality had mellowed him, I thought.

He shook my hand. 'Look all right Harry. War done someone some good then,' he added to me as a sideways compliment.

He then opened his mouth to smile and it revealed that he still refused to purchase dentures. 'Bloody useless to get fitted up with teeth when me gums can cut into an apple like an axe,' he had once remarked.

That day, however, he had no wisdom to impart to me,

except: 'It's time for a bit of quiet.' Bill Moxon then disappeared off to the outdoor privy with a newspaper.

With Moxon gone to the thunder box, my two younger brothers presumed it was safe to come into the kitchen and greet me. They looked as uncomfortable as I felt. We eyed each other up and down as dogs from different litters do. Since each of us had a different father, we recognised each other more by our differences than by any shared similarities.

Matt, the elder of my younger brothers, had grown. He was now seventeen, tall and lanky with jet-black hair and a raven's face. He looked a lot like his father, the Irish transient who was the first of many to cuckold my real father. Matt had developed into a cocky teen. He wasn't the small boy I remembered. He wasn't the wee one my sister and I used to keep a watchful eye over when our Mam was on the piss.

Matt showered a grin on me that said more about what he lacked in experience than what he had gained by learning about life on Boothtown Road. With piss and vinegar on his words, he shook my hands and said, 'How ya doing, Harry. Did you kill any Germans?'

'Sorry, mate, I killed no Germans.'

News that my war exploits lacked bloodshed and daring seemed to disappoint him. He looked downcast, but cheered up enough to ask me, 'What did you bring me back from the war?'

'I brought you Hitler's moustache,' I told him.

'Stop pulling his leg,' my mother reprimanded. 'He wants his war booty, like all of uz do.'

'Right,' I said. 'You were supposed to get this after tea, but here it is.'

I pulled from my kit bag a silver German wristwatch. It had intricate Roman numerals on its face and a new leather strap around it. Matt looked at it with wide-eyed wonder. His amazement at the timepiece convinced me that the only time he knew was when it was best to bugger off from our mother. His appreciation was laconic. 'That's all right then,' he said.

Happily and awkwardly, he put the watch onto his wrist and admired its look.

'Show me the bloody watch,' my mother belted out.

Matt walked over and our mother grabbed hold of his wrist. She eyed the watch as if she was sizing it up for a future trip to the pawn shop.

My other half-brother, Billy, stood awkwardly in the background. He was twelve and the product of too much cider and gin between Moxon and my Mam. Billy and I didn't know each other because we were a generation apart in age, experience and sentiment. Before the war, I thought he was a nuisance and an embarrassment. For me, he was more evidence of my mother's philandering irresponsibility. In our confused family hierarchy, I considered Billy to be no more significant than my pet mouse, which my mother killed by crushing it with her rocking chair leg. I don't think Billy thought any better of me; he openly said of me: 'He's not Moxon. He's a bleeding Smith problem.'

'What did ya git for junior?' Mam screamed out to me, even though we were within arm's reach.

I pulled out my wallet and handed Billy a pound note and said, 'There's your gift. That pound was given to me by Göring as war reparations. Now it's yours to spend on Mackintosh sweets.'

'Ta,' he said, fingering the note as if he were checking to see if it were counterfeit.

The excitement of my return quickly wore off on my two brothers. They hastily said their goodbyes to me and quickly left our mother's dingy house. Outside I heard them cursing all the way up the street.

With my brothers gone, my mother informed me that my sister was expected to arrive shortly.

Silently, I looked around the house while my mother sat at the kitchen table and slurped a cup of tea as viscous as treacle. It looked as if the interior of this house hadn't seen a fresh coat of paint since Queen Victoria died. My mother and the cowman couldn't afford the paint and probably reasoned, 'Why cover up what's plain for anyone to see: we live in shite.' I thought compared to Europe, Britain had the worst type of poverty. England's poor were a filthy lot kept like dogs in a shit-filled kennel by masters who should have been jailed for their cruelty and greed.

'Those two boys are a handful,' my mother lamented to me about my departed brothers. 'Shame that there's no one to ever give me a hand.'

While my mother's words ground onwards like the lamentation of Job, I lit a cigarette. I counted in my head the time left before I had to catch my train and return to Manchester and fly back to Germany.

At around seven, Mary arrived. She hugged me deeply,

repeatedly, and transferred an endless amount of love back to me. It was what I most admired about my sister, her boundless loyalty to those she loved.

'Let's have a look at you', she said. 'God, you've got big and strong on RAF food. You're not that bag of bones who said tara to me six years ago.'

'You look good too,' I replied deceitfully. Mary appeared to me as thin as a tubercular patient and had developed a strong smoker's cough.

'Bloody liar,' she retorted. 'Go on now,' she said encouragingly, 'show us a picture of this true love of yours.'

I pulled out a small snapshot of Friede, whereupon Mary cooed, 'She's right lovely, isn't she, Mam?'

My mother looked at it and snorted. 'I've seen worse. It's beyond me, lad, why you want to go and marry a bloody Nazi. You're just like thy Dad, head in the clouds, a bloody dreamer.'

'Go on now, Mam,' Mary said defensively. 'Harry's got a right to dream and be in love. There's no crime in wanting what your heart fancies.'

'Bollocks,' my mother retorted. 'The both of you I can see are from the same Da. Dreaming did him no bloody good and uz no bloody good. In this life, keep yer feet firmly planted on the bloody ground, even if you are knee-deep in shite. No dreams, no looking with milk cream eyes to the sky is going to save thee and pull thee from the muck.'

'Wasn't his fault, Mam,' Mary said in our dead father's defence. 'In those days, our only friends were bad luck and cold porridge and it weren't Dad's mistake for our fall into misery. Anyway, Mam, if our Dad was a dreamer, at least you wuz the schemer. So, no harm done, Mam, 'cause you landed us in the right tip when we wuz young.'

As the two argued and bickered, I shrank into the background. It felt like I was a ten-year-old boy again, caught between their conflicting feelings of love and hate for each other. After a while, the fires in each of them dimmed and we sat around the kitchen table. I listened to them gossip to me about my uncles and aunts and their own strange lives during the war. Before Mary left, I took out the lace handkerchief I had bought for her in Brussels. She cooed over it as she once did when we were small and I treated her to a chocolate bar.

It was time to give my mother her gift. Friede had bought her a green blown-glass fruit bowl, which looked too beautiful for this house or any fruit that might mistakenly end up in my mother's larder.

My mother opened her gift, which was wrapped in plain brown paper. Her eyes lit up as she looked at the delicate blown glass. 'Now that's real Nazi booty,' she declared.

'Crikey, Mam,' I interrupted. 'Friede bought that for you. It's not loot.'

'Wait until I show your aunties this. It's actual German war booty. They'll be gob-smacked. Bloody marvellous, it's bloody marvellous, son,' she said.

Mary whispered to me: 'Don't let the old girl down; let her believe that it's from Hitler's bunker if she wants. She's a daft old cow, but she is our Mam.'

My sister reached over and took a cigarette from my pack. She told me: 'I think your Friede is beautiful.'

'She's still a bleeding German,' my mother interjected.

'Wot's she going to do in Halifax? I don't see many jobs going for Nazis down at mills or in shops. Bet she can't even speak bloody English,' my mother said with an under-educated self-satisfaction.

'Mam, shut it,' Mary said. 'It's beautiful that Harry is going to marry a German girl. She did nothing to harm uz and you better remember that, Mam, before you go and open up yer cake-hole and say something cruel to her when you meet her.' She turned to me. 'When are you coming home with her?'

'Not for a long while I hope,' I replied thankfully.

Before my leave ended, my mother in her own emotionally amputated way tried to mend the loose and torn threads of our relationship.

'I'm right proud of ya, Harry, for bringin' yer Mam back sum war booty, right proud of you. As a peace offering,' she added. 'If you've got to go and marry a German and live your life in the clouds, try not to scrape yer knees when you tumble. There's nobody in this world that's going to catch you or me when we fall,' she said ruefully. 'It's bloody tough but there you are. It's a bloody hard life, but it's a damn sight better than resting in the dirt like yer Dad.'

CHAPTER 23

A pawn takes a bishop

By 1947, I had lived through several springs in Germany and experienced two of their most brutal winters. Hamburg was still pursued by three furies – chaos, corruption and destruction – that held on to the city like a pack of crazed Alsatians. There was little difference in any other part of Germany because reconstruction moved at a meandering evolutionary pace. On many occasions, German economic and spiritual renewal regressed as it struggled through the avenues of incompetence, myopia and avarice. Human nature being what it is, it didn't surprise me that the new Germany was built on the foundations of their old evils and temptations. In each individual community, success and growth depended on the kinship that benevolence shares with malevolence, or greed with charity. Even the economic union Bizonia, launched in the winter months between the American and British sectors, was slow going.

Commerce between the two zones was blighted by power blackouts, capital shortages, and theft. It was profoundly worrisome that the rest of western Europe was infected by this same financial and spiritual malaise. It was clear to anyone that the Continent was broken from Lublin to Lombardy. The infrastructure, from bridges to ports, factories and warehouses, was either destroyed or in such disrepair that the owners had abandoned it to be reclaimed by nature. The inhabitants weren't much better off and most populations struggled with incessant food shortages.

Two years after the Second World War ended, Europe's attrition became a grave concern to the United States. Their worry was echoed by journalists, academics and writers, who feared the whole European continent was tumbling into the Soviet sphere of influence through neglect and poor planning. George Marshall, the American Secretary of State, proposed a radical solution in June 1947. The US was going to rebuild and feed Europe on low-interest, long-term American loans. He believed bankrolling Europe wasn't charity but good commerce. A financially sound Continent was more likely to be democratic, pro-capitalist, and eager to buy American manufactured goods. Cash and common sense were his only weapons against the Soviet allure of equality among men and the collectivisation of wealth.

I wasn't sure if Europe had had its chips, but I was getting scared that my day was done if the RAF didn't give me permission to marry. My greatest fear was being demobbed back home before the event, because I was on my last permissible six-month extension and it was due to expire in the autumn.

Through most of June, I fretted and sweated over my predicament. Flight Lieutenant Locke had no answers for me. I was advised to 'Keep a stiff upper lip, Smith.' He intimated that I must accept the karma of military life: 'It will come when it will come.'

By the end of the month, and a year since I began my journey to marry Friede, word was sent to me to meet with my commanding officer. His adjutant, Flight Lieutenant

Locke, was also in attendance at the meeting. I didn't know how the conference was going to unfold, but I did feel self-assured because both Cox and Locke were fair and decent men. Cox flipped through a file on his desk. It was my dossier that possessed every document pertaining to my service with the RAF and my year-long quest to marry a German girl.

Cox looked up from the papers and said with sincerity, 'I must congratulate you, LAC Smith. You have confounded and defeated the RAF with your diligence to paperwork. It gives me great pleasure to inform you that as far as the Air Ministry is concerned, you are free to marry your fiancée, Elfriede Giselle Edelmann.' Cox looked as relieved as me that everything had apparently worked out for the best.

'At the beginning of this odyssey,' the group captain said, 'I mentioned to you that you were the first under my command to request marriage to a German woman. I am pleased that you succeeded where many others would have given up on this mighty challenge. It demonstrates that you are of good character.'

'Thank you, sir.'

Locke interjected: 'Good show, Smith.'

I thought I was about to be dismissed when Cox coughed and added: 'There is one more issue we must discuss: your status in the RAF. I have been informed that you are scheduled to be demobbed in the forthcoming months. So I must caution you to get this wedding over with, on the double. You don't want to get shipped home without your wife-to-be.'

The group captain was correct. Efficiency dictated that

my marriage ceremony be a quick affair. However, I had concocted a plan to keep me in Germany and in the pay of the RAF for a long while. I was simply going to re-enlist into the RAF for their standard three-year tour. I decided not to tell the group captain until after my wedding. I feared he would cashier me out of the services if he knew I wanted to stay in Hamburg with a German national for a wife.

I replied to Cox that I intended to get married in August.

'That is cutting it a bit short,' interjected the adjutant.

'I know, sir, but we want a church wedding and I am RC.'

'Oh,' he noted, as if I had confessed to necromancy.

'I thought almost everyone nowadays has a civil ceremony,' he commented.

'My fiancée wants a religious wedding service,' I explained.

'I think you should talk to the padre about that,' said the group captain. 'It really isn't my speciality. I am sure he can round up a man with a Catholic dog collar.'

'Perhaps to expedite matters, sir,' the adjutant interjected, 'we could ask the vicar. He might be able to arrange a meeting for LAC Smith with someone in authority at the Roman Catholic Church in Hamburg.' The group captain thought this a very good idea.

Before I was dismissed, Cox noted that the RAF was doing everything for my wedding but throwing me a night out with the lads.

I thanked both officers for their support and left the office elated. Once I had finished my duties in the communications tower, I rushed straight to Friede's apartment. When I told Friede our good news, she kissed me passionately.

'Finally,' she said, 'we are to be married. I won't believe it until we are truly wed in a church. I won't tell anyone but Mutti until we have spoken to a priest and arranged the day.'

'It is coming soon,' I reassured her. Silently, I dreaded what the reception was going to cost, and what would happen if I was demobbed prematurely.

One week later, I was called in to see our base padre, Chaplain Walker. He was a youngish man with a kind face. He seemed genuinely concerned for his flock. Walker greeted me in a warm and friendly voice. 'I've had a spot of good luck and was able to arrange a meeting for you and your fiancée with the Catholic bishop who governs this parish.'

He flipped through some notes on a pad of paper and added: 'Oh yes, here it is: the bishop is Wilhelm Berning von Osnabrück. Try saying that three times,' Walker remarked good-naturedly.

'The bishop doesn't live in Hamburg but told me he is prepared to meet you in the city at Pastor Wintermann's residence. He is a monsignor with the church. The bishop wants to discuss with you your intention to marry this German woman,' the padre added with a note of dismay.

'What is there to discuss?' I asked suspiciously.

Walker nervously laughed and explained: 'I think perhaps you know the Germans better than me. Your bishop has some bee in his bonnet, but he wasn't about to reveal any secrets to me.' The padre wrote the address and appointment time on a scrap of paper and handed it to me.

When I was about to leave, the padre wished me luck and warned me. 'Smith, I know you are RC.'

Not by much, I thought.

'But I must advise you that having spoken with this bishop, he is a bit of a character.'

'What do you mean?' I asked.

'Well, for starters, he is one of the most disagreeable persons I have ever encountered in Germany. I've asked around and the man wasn't a Nazi per se, but he certainly doesn't believe in a democratic modern society. My impression was that he still has a bone to pick with Luther for the Reformation.'

'I see,' I said.

'One last thing,' Walker added. 'My final impression of the bishop is of a man who doesn't accept dissent. I think he still believes in pitchforks, devils, and the fiery bowels of hell. Remember, fools rush in where angels fear to tread. Be careful what you say and do while in the company of the bishop. Let me know how it turns out for you. I am always here to help if something goes amiss.'

Several days later, Friede and I went to meet the bishop. Friede dressed as reverentially as possible in a plain long cotton dress with dowdy shoes. I wore my best uniform.

Pastor Wintermann's residence was located in a prosperous neighbourhood in the northern part of the city. We came to his door and I rang the bell with trepidation. To my surprise, the monsignor answered his own door. He let us in to a large hallway, whose walls were covered in small pictures of saints and church leaders. Wintermann informed me that the bishop was upstairs in his office. We were led to the second floor by Wintermann. Our footsteps on the staircase were cushioned by an ancient Persian carpet runner. The interior of the house was cast in gloomy dark colours. It was as quiet as a funeral parlour, except for the annoying heavy sounds coming from the mechanical parts of old clocks in desperate need of lubrication.

Wintermann knocked and announced us. I walked into the room holding Friede's hand. The curtains were drawn as if sunlight were a sin and an impediment to ecclesiastical work. The monsignor was like a mute assistant to a medieval inquisition. He gestured for us to sit in two chairs positioned before a large desk. Behind it sat the bishop, who ignored our entrance and continued working strenuously on some composition. He was dressed as a simple priest and was around 60 with thinning white hair.

Friede and I sat close together holding each other's hands. After some time, the bishop looked up from his writings and took off his reading glasses. 'And you are?' he asked with prosecutorial skill.

The bishop was perfectly aware of our identities and purpose, but I indulged his charade and told him our names and our reason for being before him. At the start of our interview, he spoke exclusively to Friede. His tone was supercilious, but seemed harmless. He concerned himself with knowing more about where she was born and baptised, the schools she went to, and where she now lived. The bishop spoke to her for no more than five minutes and then dismissed her.

'Child, please wait outside. I must discuss some matters with your fiancé.'

I wanted to protest, but sheepishly let the bishop remove Friede from the room. Once the heavy door was safely closed, the bishop clasped his hands together and remained in a trance of contemplation or contempt for my presence. 'Your Excellency,' I asked, 'does the church have an issue with my wish to be married?'

'There is no issue for you, my son,' the bishop said. 'You are Catholic. Perhaps you are not particularly pious, but you are a Catholic. Where the problem lies is with that woman, your fiancée. She is not Catholic and I know she is certainly not pious.'

In his condescending tone, the bishop outlined his reservations about my marriage to Friede. The Catholic church in Germany, he explained, was under attack by modern forces that had undermined its moral authority. From the moment the Kaiser abdicated in 1918, Germany, according to the bishop, had begun to decay and rot inside, from every venial and mortal sin. It was his duty to God, to his church, and to his country to stop this decay before it permanently ruined the German people.

'I cannot bless this marriage union between you and that German girl,' he said.

If he were to sanction my marriage, the bishop reasoned, he was inviting sin to flourish in Germany. To marry this woman was an affront to the Catholic church and its beliefs. I sat with my back ramrod straight against an uncomfortable wooden seat. I listened to his homily and held my tongue until he reached the apogee of his argument.

'You must be strong, my son, and accept my wisdom and

decision. I shall not sanction your marriage to that woman now or ever.'

'Why?' I asked indignantly.

'I have read about Elfriede Edelmann's background. She is illegitimate. Her mother is illegitimate, and compounded her sin by living for many years with a man out of wedlock. This profane life is not acceptable to the church. These people,' he continued, as if they were less than animals, 'are unfit to be called Germans let alone be allowed into the Catholic faith.'

'Your Excellency,' I started, my hands crushed tightly against the armrest of my chair in an attempt to hold the anger growing within me. 'This is impossible. My fiancée is not immoral.'

The bishop unfolded his hands and replied: 'You are young and naive. I say this with a heavy heart, but Nazism and Hitler turned German women into licentious wanton women.'

He pointed past the shut curtains and said in a measured tone: 'Hamburg is a city of prostitutes and I am afraid you have been duped because the only German girl who wants to marry an occupying soldier is a prostitute.'

If I had had the courage, I would have struck him down and bashed in his smug head. Instead, I fell into a contemptuous laughter for this man and the ridiculous church he served. 'Your Excellency, I will marry her.'

'It is impossible, the church forbids it.'

'You forbid it,' I retorted.

'Rome shall forbid it. Do you wish me to seek their guidance?' he asked as if wagering me.

'I am afraid I don't have years to waste on silly ecclesiastical squabbles. So I shall marry her and I don't care what the church thinks.'

The bishop rose from his seat as if he were a mountain lion waiting to leap onto his prey. 'If you marry her without the church's blessing, you are on the path towards excommunication and eternal damnation from Jesus Christ, our lord and saviour.'

It was my turn to stand and I addressed the bishop. 'Your Excellency, if the church believes this woman to be evil and a threat to it, I gladly accept excommunication. I am not afraid of eternal damnation because before I met Friede, I was in hell. She is my salvation. So sod you and sod your bleeding church.'

I left the room and met Friede downstairs and we walked hurriedly out into the fresh air of the street. 'What happened?' she asked with worry in her voice. 'Is everything OK? Did I do something wrong in there?'

'You, my love, did nothing wrong in there. Unfortunately, I was the problem. The esteemed bishop believes I'm not a good Catholic and not a good match for you. He won't condone a marriage between an immoral British soldier and a good German girl. So I'm afraid I made a bit of a mess of it.'

We stopped walking and stood close together on the pavement. I looked into Friede's eyes and spoke. 'So I ask you again, will you marry me, even if the Catholic church thinks I am a bad and fallen man?'

Friede gripped my hand and replied: 'I am yours for ever. What a silly church to think you are a bad man.'

'It's a stupid church, isn't it,' I agreed.

'But who will marry us then?' Friede asked, perplexed.

I laughed and told her: 'I have it on good authority that God runs a couple of other churches that might be willing to accept me as a member.'

CHAPTER 24

The witch before the wedding

The summer dragged on from one humid day to the
next. When July melted into August, Hamburg was
as comfortable as a blast furnace. The sky above us was an
endless pastel blue that was broken only by the jet stream
from RAF transport planes. No one escaped the heatwave
beating down on the city from sunrise to sunset. Even the
street hustlers, prostitutes and black marketeers looked for
relief and decamped to cooler surroundings.

During those uncomfortable dog days of summer,
cafés along the Alster advertised chilled beer, ice cream
and umbrellas to shield their patrons from the sun. The
water on the artificial lake behind the Malcolm Club grew
tepid and stagnant. The depth of the reservoir shrank
as it evaporated into the atmosphere. Punters beached
themselves in the middle of the basin as if they were near
the shore.

Night time was just as unbearable as the day because
there was no breeze and the air was thick and heavy as lard.
The act of breathing was as uncomfortable as inhaling the
hot atmosphere behind a closed oven door. Many evenings,
Friede and her mother took to the balcony for respite from
the inferno inside the apartment and cooled themselves with
colourful Chinese fans and drank white wine until the early
morning hours. Now that all formalities and official requests

had been met, the two women finalised plans for the wedding, set for the sixteenth of August.

The base padre made good on his word and proved that he was always a friend for those in need. When he found out about the Catholic bishop's displeasure at my marriage, he said: 'Those Germans sometimes make a lot of bother over nothing. I have a simple solution to your dilemma: it would be my pleasure to officiate at your wedding and conduct a Church of England service.'

I said it was no trouble for me and thought he could have married us in a voodoo ceremony if it got the job done.

Wisely, he suggested that we use a Lutheran church called St Luke's for our wedding ceremony because it was only blocks away from Friede's mother's apartment. Considering that our reception was scheduled to be held at Maria Edelmann's residence, it was a perfect solution. The chaplain recommended that we pay a call on the pastor to thank him for lending us St Luke's for our wedding.

A week before our marriage, Friede and I went to see him. As a token of our appreciation, I gave the minister some coffee to be used for trade on the black market. He thanked me and to my surprise greeted Friede as one of his flock. It was a revelation for me to discover that while I slept late on Sunday mornings, Friede frequented the church to listen to the parson's sermons.

The Lutheran was delighted at being able to volunteer his church for our marriage. The old pastor displayed a great deal of affection for Friede and presented her with a copy of the New Testament. Inside the book, he wrote an inscription to remind her of her faith and her fatherland. Friede handed it to me and I smiled politely and flipped through the pages with as much interest as if it were Sanskrit or excerpts from the Egyptian Book of the Dead. I returned the Testament to her without a word. I knew that my keepsake was Friede because she was my love, my faith, and my homeland.

My understanding of marriage rituals was slim, and Friede had to remind me that I required a best man. At the last moment, I asked Sid if he would fulfil the function. 'S'all right by me,' he said.

The only other person from base that I invited to the wedding was Dave. All of the other invited guests were Friede's family and friends. On the night before the wedding, I attended a Polterabend with Friede. The Polterabend was a Germanic pre-wedding celebration. The custom dated back to a dark, primal time when Germany was covered in forest and its inhabitants were savage tribes who waged war and made love in pagan excess.

The ritual combined large amounts of drinking, witchcraft, dancing, singing, and smashed crockery. When I arrived at Friede's mother's apartment, it was standing room only. It seemed everyone on the street had shown up to wish us well. I walked from one room to the next, squeezing between people as if I were an animal penned for the butcher. Hands slapped my back while others tried to shake my hand. Women kissed my cheek and men tried to top up my wine glass. The temperature inside the apartment was tropical, and the male guests poured shots of schnapps and begged me to join them. In the hallway, outside the apartment, women danced to music coming from a gramophone.

'Come drink with us,' they beckoned, but I shook my head and politely declined.

When darkness fell, a neighbour dressed as a medieval witch came to the party, complete with broom in hand. In a great barking voice, she evacuated the apartment and pushed the drunken revellers to the outside of the building. She commanded the gods of the forest and the gods of the mountains to help us achieve a life rich in promise, security and love. One by one, the guests took an old plate, bowl, or cup they had brought with them from home and smashed it against the threshold of the apartment's entrance, making ribald jokes as the crockery broke into a myriad of pieces.

Everyone laughed when someone shouted out that more crockery was broken that night than in all of the British air raids during the war. One after the other, friend, family, or neighbour went to the entrance and dropped their plate, shattering it on the concrete. The ground was littered with shards of tableware. The witch urged more destruction and demanded that a chamber pot be crushed to give a lifetime of happiness and good luck to us.

Friede and I were in the crowd standing together arm-in-arm, when the hag approached and drank from each of our wine glasses. 'I have now blessed your life in the tradition of the woodland gods,' the witch said, slurring her words. 'Prosit,' she called out to everyone, who returned her toast.

I was told that each glass of wine drunk that night was a good wish upon our marriage. It was an irreverent consecration by her family and friends and I welcomed it as sincere.

It was something I wasn't accustomed to seeing back in Britain, where we concealed our joy as much as our pain.

Later on, the retired sea captain who lived in the top-floor apartment brought out his accordion and serenaded us with waltzes and polkas. Near the end of the festivities, I was commanded by the witch to sweep the stoop clean of the shards of broken dishes.

'You must know who is in charge,' cackled the witch. 'Friedl is now your master. Treat her well through this life and you will be rewarded with the riches of a hundred kings,' she announced, before downing her last glass of wine and stumbling homewards.

The party lasted many hours. Near its end, the guests lingered and drank the last dregs of wine and beer. They shared shag cigarettes and memories of their own Polterabend.

Just before midnight, I kissed Friede goodnight. I was slightly drunk and very happy. 'The next time I see you,' I said, 'we'll be at the church. I can hardly believe I'm to be a married man, to you, the most wonderful, beautiful person on this planet.'

'Hush,' she said and put a finger close to my lips. 'It is only you who I love or will ever love. You are now my life and my love, but go because tomorrow we shall be wed.'

CHAPTER 25

16 August 1947

On the way back to camp, I quietly sang to myself the song 'I'm the Man Who Broke the Bank at Monte Carlo'. When I returned to my quarters, I was surprised to find that Sid and Dave had broken in and were waiting for me with a bottle of whisky.

Dave said, 'I'd been saving this for a special occasion and since nothing came around, I thought why not drink it tonight.'

So my two friends and I drank whisky and toasted our old lives together. Sid told me: 'You did all right, Harry. Didn't get much loot out of Germany, but you did steal the prettiest girl.'

'That I did,' I replied.

'What happens now to you and Friede?' Dave asked.

I told them that RAF regulations required servicemen who married a foreign national be provided accommodation off base. 'I'll be chuffed,' said Sid.

'It's a brilliant set-up.' I explained that Friede and I were allotted rooms in a beautiful house, ten minutes from the base. The rent and all our living supplies would be paid by the RAF.

'I wouldn't let that get out,' Dave warned me, 'or everyone in the RAF is going to marry a German girl, just for the housing.'

'Harry, you and Friede deserve it. Best of luck,' Sid toasted me. 'Now we'd better be off or else you'll be over-sleeping on your wedding day.'

That night I didn't sleep much due to the wine, the heat, and the anticipation of the wedding. Until the sun rose, I endured restless and disquieting dreams. I was relieved to be awake and away from my subconscious, which was like a cemetery where too many corpses were buried in shallow graves. In my dreams, I saw my Dad's sad face. I wasn't sure if the dream was wishing me well or warning me of rough times ahead.

Whether the dreams were omens or glad tidings, I real-ised that I still had to prepare for my wedding and ensure that all the food and drink were available for the recep-tion. For a hefty bribe, I had made arrangements with the camp cook to provide all the food for the feast, from cakes to exquisite sandwiches. The three-tier wedding cake was made by a pastry chef attached to the NAAFI in Hamburg. Everything for the wedding reception was transported in on an RAF truck and delivered for 10.00am. I had press-ganged some other servicemen with promises of beer on a later date to help unload and set up the banquet tables, chairs, food and flowers for the reception. Everything was assembled in Maria Edelmann's oversized bedroom as it was the only suitable space to fit 25 guests.

While we got to work putting the room together, Friede argued with her mother, who was arranging her hair and assisting with her make-up in the Gellersons' room.

Frau Gellerson said to me: 'You must be quick and go; it is bad luck to see the bride in the morning before your wedding.'

I left as quickly as I could. On my way out, I saw the men from the Malcolm Club deliver a giant keg of beer; they struggled to take it down to the cellar, where it could be kept cool during the sweltering August afternoon.

With haste, I returned to camp to get cleaned up for the ceremony. As I dressed, I started to shake and had to sit down and have a cigarette. I was overcome by my good fortune and the fear it was going to run out. How is it possible, I asked myself, that I fell into this joy, this great promise of better days? I didn't know the reason except blind luck. There were so many others who missed out on life and were cut down before their time because of the Great Depression or the war. Yet I had somehow survived. I was granted by fortune or endurance or whimsy the chance to love and be loved in return. I had arrived at the entrance to a life worth living. 'Don't bugger it up,' I said while brushing my hair tightly back.

When Stan and I rode up to the church in a jeep, I saw there was a growing crowd of inquisitive onlookers loitering around the entrance. Stan and I quickly rushed through the church doors and passed the assembled guests as we moved towards the altar. While I waited for Friede, Stan cracked jokes to me and the vicar.

It was hot inside the church and the air was stagnant. The padre was sweating and the organist looked uncomfortable on his stool. I mopped my brow with a handkerchief; Stan said, 'Hope none of the neighbours nick the beer while we're at church.'

After several more perspiring moments, I heard the doors open at the back of St Luke's. The guests shuffled in

245

their seats and then made an appreciative collective sigh. Friede had arrived with her foster father, Max. The music was struck and Friede walked slowly towards me. I knew that she was drinking in this moment. I knew that every step Friede took, she believed was a final and absolute negation of her stigma. Walking up that aisle, she wasn't just coming towards me; she was walking away from her childhood sorrows, pains and humiliations. I wanted to turn around, but dared not. Stan glanced backwards and whispered to me, 'Blimey, she's beautiful.'

Finally, Friede and Max were beside us. The organ notes faded away like a feather caught in a breeze. Max ceremoniously relinquished Friede to my care. He whispered in my ear: 'Be well and remember to be tender to my Friedl.'

Friede and I sheepishly smiled at each other. She whispered the words, 'Ich liebe dich.' The silk bridal gown magnified her loveliness and made her beauty appear timeless, untouchable, and seductive. Her beauty, her history, and her fragility humbled me as I stood in my RAF blue dress uniform. Friede held a bouquet of wild flowers, whose scent perfumed the air around us. It was a wonderful fresh aroma that made me think of our time walking in the botanical gardens.

Our wedding service wasn't long but it was charged with emotion, laughter and human kindness. The chaplain joined us as man and wife, but said this was also a marriage unique for this town and for our garrison. It was the first post-war marriage between a Brit and a German. It was a signal, he said. It was a harbinger of peaceful days to come because if love could germinate between two young people from different cultures, the world was healing its wounds from the war. Finally, the vicar pronounced us man and wife. He blessed the union and we were wed.

Friede and I walked slow and steady to the church's exit and on our way out, we received the adulation from the pews. I whispered a 'thank you' to Friede. She smiled and had tears in her eyes. For a brief second, I felt afraid of my new responsibility and I hoped I wouldn't disappoint her. I didn't want to muddle up destiny's kindness towards me.

On the steps of the church, a wedding photographer took our picture. Once the pictures were taken, the guests were ferried to the reception in a fleet of Volkswagen taxis I had commandeered earlier on in the day for a hefty black-market bribe.

The feast, the feelings of good will, and the emotional atmosphere were never better at Maria Edelmann's apartment than on the day of our reception. Everyone was content; no one brought any disgruntled and disjointed emotions to the party. There were toasts from Friede's mother. There were speeches from Sid and Dave. Congratulatory telegrams arrived from my mother and sister. Friede translated them into German and read them out to the guests, who applauded my English family for their warm-hearted support.

We drank wine and beer, and ate cakes and delicate sandwiches. Cigarettes were shared and hands held. I felt proud that I had orchestrated this feast of love for Friede, her family and her friends. Half-way through the reception, Friede slipped out of the room. She quickly returned and sat beside her mother. They talked in low voices and then hugged each other warmly. Friede walked over to a painting hanging on the wall and placed a small wallet-sized photo of her father Fritz along the edges of the frame. She raised her glass and announced:

'To my mother who loved me in dangerous times; to my foster mother for caring for me; to my foster father who loved me as his own.' The wedding table broke into applause at the dedications. When the clapping stopped, Friede continued: 'I raise my glass to Harry, who will love me until the end of days, and I shall love him whether the sea is in storm or the waters calm.'

CHAPTER 26

The end of the party

For the first few days following my wedding, the skies above Hamburg remained clear, blue and peaceful. The summer held us in her grip and it was sunny and humid; time stood to catch its breath. I quickly grew accustomed to life as a married man with a bit of status and wealth, compliments of the RAF. I was having too much of a good time to notice the ominous threats all around me. Sometimes in the afternoons, I heard the rumble of thunder far off in the distance, but Hamburg remained sweltering and dry. It will never reach us, I thought. The summer will continue well into October, I reasoned. Even when the winter comes, I dreamed, life will be grand in this new house. We will sit by a roaring fire while a roast chicken cooks in the oven.

I believed I had a long life coming to me, which was to be spent in Hamburg. I had it all planned and measured out. We would live in this requisitioned house for a couple of years. Friede and I were going to loaf from one lazy summer day to the next down at the Malcolm Club, getting drunk on lager and youthful desires. We were going to enjoy life and after my time with the RAF was over, I was going to find a trade that would make us comfortable and secure.

Those days we spent in our new house on Bergkoppelweg gave me a sense of serenity and comfort I had never experienced in my entire life. It was a suburban, almost posh address and it was a home designed for someone well-placed in the middle class. We shared the house with the owner, a widow, and her daughter, who occupied the upstairs rooms. Friede and I lived very comfortably on the lower floor, where our bedroom overlooked a well-tended back garden. The basement was reserved for the owner's dachshund and her litter of puppies. The mother and her pups scampered through the house as if they were the true owners who graciously allowed us to stay with them.

In between my work at the base, we threw dinner parties and drank wine in the garden until late in the evening. At nights when Friede and I were alone, we shared cigarettes and watched the sun sink behind the linden trees and disappear into the horizon. I was unconscious to the danger of change. My new marriage and carte blanche life lulled me into a euphoric state as dreamlike as a body injected with morphine.

One night as I undressed and folded my clothes, placing them in the giant wardrobe in our bedroom, I was stung by an insect.

'What is it?' Friede asked in a sleepy voice from the bed.

'Nothing,' I responded, 'just a bloody midge.'

At first, the bite wasn't anything to be concerned about; it was red, itchy, and a nuisance. However, by the following morning, Friede said, 'You should have it looked at.'

I said, 'Nonsense, it's just a scratch. Let's enjoy our breakfast out on the front porch before I leave for the base.'

Days passed, friends dropped by and every night was a

party at our new dwelling. However, the small bite on my arm grew septic and I fell into a fever. A fortnight after my wedding and a week after the mosquito had supped on my blood, I was rushed to hospital chattering and delirious. I almost went mad from the insect's venomous bite. For two nights, I lay in a parallel state in that country bordering life and death. Doctors pumped my body full of newly invented antibiotics. Friede remained at my side, but in my fever I didn't recognise her and screamed and babbled like a man taken by senility or drink.

While I was hospitalised, Friede was frightened that her days as a bride were numbered. She asked her mother: 'Is this what happens to all the Edelmann women? Must we always end up alone and abandoned?'

Eventually, the medicine took hold; the sweating, the fever, the delusions and the terror were purged from my body. Yet when I was discharged from the infirmary, I felt that my recent brush with mortality was a sign that my run of good luck was rapidly coming to its end.

I returned to work at the airport's telecommunications tower during the second week of September and a sergeant reminded me: 'You'll be demobbed next month, Smith. Hope you've got a fancy house back in England for your new missus.'

The snide comment was like an electric cattle prod to remind me that not everyone wished me well or thought my situation was proper. The following day, I went to the adjutant officer's secretary to see if I could make an appointment with Flight Lieutenant Locke. The adjutant officer had recently replaced his secretary. The new gatekeeper was an offensive prim boy who wanted to make himself a name in the RAF through slander, innuendo, and trading in false rumours.

When I arrived, the secretary berated me as if he were an officer. 'Can't be always coming and going to see the adjutant,' he said to me. 'Really, you see the man more than his wife does. It's just not proper.'

'Why don't you just stick to making the tea and bringing the biscuits,' I told him sarcastically.

'What is the nature of your meeting?'

'I wish to join the peace-time RAF.'

'Aren't you the patriot?' he said, making notes.

Fuck off, I thought, and replied: 'Oi, chop to it and put me in for an appointment with the adjutant.'

'Well, I'll try to slot you in before you are demobbed, but the Flight Lieutenant is a busy man, you know.'

A week later, I got my meeting with the adjutant, who had a stern and displeased look on his face.

'Are you sure you want to sign on for three years, LAC Smith? It's a long tour. You have been an excellent member of the RAF during wartime and during this occupation. However, I'm not sure you're made for a long career in the Royal Air Force.'

'Sir, I believe I am just the type of man suited for the RAF.'

'This has nothing to do with your recent marriage?' he asked cynically.

'No,' I said.

Locke looked at me as if I was a fool and recanted. 'I will approve it with reluctance. Remember, you're signing away your life for three years and you are ours to do with as we wish.'

'I know.' I wasn't going to tell the adjutant, but I had read the contract beforehand. In the fine print, there was a buy-out clause that could be initiated within the first six months of the contract. For £20, if things got unbearable with the RAF, I could walk away and learn to be a civilian again.

When Sid found out, he screamed at me: 'You big bloody fool! They are going to give you a bollocking like you have never imagined.'

'Perhaps,' I said, 'but I had no other recourse to stay on in Germany.'

I went back home to Friede that night and told her what I had done. She was relieved, but still had as many misgivings as Sid. 'Let's hope it works out for us,' she said, 'and if not, then we hold on until the bad weather has passed.'

Later on that night, I found her crying and she confessed that she didn't want to leave Germany and her family.

When the contract took effect, I was now no longer a draftee, but a regular. I had moved from amateur to professional with the stroke of a pen. At first, nothing changed for me in either my work duties or how I was treated. I began to believe I'd dodged another bullet. I started to think that I had outfoxed the Air Ministry and was going to remain in Fuhlsbüttel for another ten years. I was a fool to be so optimistic. The moment I signed on for three more years in the RAF, plans from above were in motion to remove me from Fuhlsbüttel.

In late September, I was called in to see the adjutant

officer. It was a brief meeting. It lasted no more than three minutes and Flight Lieutenant Locke's eyes never met mine. 'You have been transferred to Lübeck. You are to report there tomorrow morning. So you must take the train tonight.'

It was like being punched in the stomach and not being allowed to cry out. 'Might I ask why I am being transferred?' I asked, as if the reason mattered.

'Because the RAF wants you there,' Locke replied in a fed-up tone.

'What about my wife?'

Locke said succinctly: 'That is your problem, not ours. Naturally, for the time being she can remain at the lodgings provided her, but that may change at any moment.'

I left the office and went to tell Sid about my transfer. 'I told you, they are never going to let an enlisted man stay in Germany with a wife and a home. It sets a bad example that every punter can get a chance for happiness. Buy yourself out, Harry, and get back to England. Jump man, jump back into the real world, shite as it is, before it's too late.'

When I told Friede, she took the news well enough. 'It is not so bad; we can see each other on weekends and if you are there long enough, we can find a house in Lübeck.'

I didn't have the courage to tell her that I feared the move was just the first in a series. I knew the RAF was just toying with me until I jumped back into the civilian world and the unemployment line in Britain.

When I arrived in Lübeck, I found there was very little for me to do but try to be scarce. It was a humiliation for me. I was returned to my earlier days in the RAF when I had no privileges. I bunked with new recruits in a Nissen hut. I ate my meals alone in the mess house and found the days friendless and long. On weekends, I was allowed to return to Hamburg and visit Friede and stay in our house.

By my second week in Lübeck, I understood that my number was up. Sergeants yelled at me for imaginary infractions. 'You might do that in Fuhlsbüttel, but here in Lübeck we follow the King's regulations.'

The berating and belittling continued for almost two months. Finally, I was called before the commanding officer for Lübeck. He looked me up and down like I was an orphaned pit pony. 'The RAF doesn't require your services any more in Germany,' he said definitively. 'You've been transferred to Manchester. It's effective immediately.'

'But, sir, I am married.'

'You'll be glad to see the wife when you're back in Britain, then.'

'No, sir, my wife is in Hamburg.'

'Oh,' he noted, 'that's right. You were the one who went off half-cocked and married a German. Take 72 hours to make good on your transfer to Manchester,' he told me.

I was given three days to say goodbye to Friede and start a life in England without her. There wasn't even time to say goodbye to my mates or most of her family as I made the dash back to Hamburg for the final time.

CHAPTER 27

Manchester 1947

I t was dawn in late November when I left Hamburg. On the horizon, strands of smoky grey clouds jostled against the dark sky. Winter had begun to creep through the city and a light frost covered the ground. I slipped away from our home on cat paws while Friede was asleep, looking lost in a pleasant dream. For the last time, I walked dejectedly on the path to the airport. The guard at the gate lazily waved me into the still half-asleep Air Force base. I didn't look left or right or back through the camp gates; I just made my way to embarkation. There I stood in a pencil-thin line waiting to board a Dakota, back to Britain.

'Oi, it looks like it's going to snow,' said the teenage RAF recruit standing behind me.

I grunted, yes or no or maybe. I didn't care because it was colder, wetter and more inhospitable where I was going than right now on this tarmac. The queue moved slowly towards the aircraft. When it was my turn, I put my hand on the stepladder and climbed through the fuselage's hatchway.

The DC-3 was already loaded with men. They sat hunched on wooden benches that skirted both sides of the plane's interior. The centre of the plane was stacked with sacks of mail, documents, and loot. I slung my kitbag underneath my legs. It didn't contain much: pictures of Friede, my spare uniforms and some cartons of cigarettes.

A sergeant came on board to do a head count. When he was satisfied, he called out: 'Strap yourself in, lads, the pilots tell me it's going to be a rough flight. So, say cheerio to Germany because you lucky sods are going home.'

The prop engines awoke to life like a coal miner in the morning, with a wheeze and a phlegmy sputtering cough. While we taxied across the runway, gathering speed for takeoff, I turned my head around and stared out the port-hole window. Violently, the pilot thrust the plane's throttle forward and we jerked into the air, gulping altitude like it was oxygen to an asthmatic.

In no time, the airport disappeared from view. For a brief moment, the plane dipped over my house on the deserted Bergkoppelweg. I put my hand against the port-hole as if I could reach out and touch my old life. Then it was gone from sight as we banked and swept over the city of Hamburg. From above, the metropolis resembled an ancient city, abandoned to the elements and to the mob. Cooking fires from the refugee camps smouldered below while the gutted docklands and working-class districts slowly began to awaken from their uncomfortable slumber. A U-Bahn train departed the Bahnhof station and cut across the shattered city, moving eastward towards Berlin, another broken city.

As we climbed into clouds pregnant with snow, the land-scape escaped my grasp. I turned away from the window and pulled out a flask of tea and whisky. I sipped on it to warm my body, while my hands shook in unison to the engine's vibration. For a few brief seconds, the cockpit door swung open and slammed shut in the turbulence. Soon we were over the cold North Sea. I closed my eyes and let the monotonous hum of the engines lull me into an unhappy sleep.

When I arrived at Gatwick, an NCO scanned my transfer orders and said, 'You better get a move on if you want to kip in Manchester tonight.'

'Why?'

'Problems on the rails,' he explained, 'because of snow, sleet and shite. Everything's buggered and you're not travelling on the Flying Scotsman.'

I looked up at the grey light streaking from the damp, heavy sky and knew he was right.

I saluted him and disappeared into the main terminal building to find a urinal. Standing beside me in the WC was a fellow Yorkshireman.

'Nivva mind t'bus, I've getten to drive van in ter tawn.'

He took me to Piccadilly. While darting through traffic and dodging a stalled double-decker bus, the driver said I was lucky to be heading to the Midlands.

'At least ya can smell 'ome from there.'

I lied to him with a smile.

I grabbed my bag and hopped out of the van, disappearing into the train station. It was choked with disgruntled commuters. I stood in front of a departure and arrival board. It clattered like old women shuffling their chairs at a boarding house. I inhaled London's desperation. It was a heavy collective breath of poverty and confusion as our empire crumbled like a limestone cliff into the sea. All around me were men wearing dirty mackintosh coats with bloodless ashen faces. They slithered between women with cheeks beaten red from the wind or Woolworths' cosmetics.

Everyone in the station had a defeated look of life lived on a ration-book existence.

At the train platform for Manchester a locomotive rested like a tired beast, panting soot and sweating filthy water down the sides of its engine carriage. A conductor read my travel warrant card and pointed me to the second-to-last car. Inside, it was standing room only. I followed the flow of heads covered with grimy hats and scarves to the middle of the train where I leaned against a dirty window.

My train dragged itself out of London like a hungover drunk. While we churned slowly northwards, snow hit the window behind me. Immediately, it turned into grimy black tears that streaked down the glass and obscured the world beyond. I was crushed up beside a middle-aged man. His face was obscured behind the pages of the *Daily Mail.* Its creased and ruffled front cover announced the partition of Palestine. The broadsheet warned that the weather was to get colder, uglier, and more inhospitable as the days moved towards Christmas. I turned away from the man wedged into his newspaper and felt nauseous from hunger and sad, unpleasant memories.

When we arrived in Manchester, I was knackered. I clambered out of the train with the other passengers like sweating livestock. Trying to make my way anonymously out of the station, a portly woman with thick glasses and bow legs accosted me.

"Scuse me, luv, got a light?' With a sigh, she rested her handbags beside me. She pulled the fag end of a cigarette out of her purse. I lit it with my Zippo.

'Flash lighter,' she noted and fell into a coughing fit.

I walk to the bus stop and asked a conductor, 'Which bus takes me to Ringwell RAF base?'

With blackened teeth and a wry grin, he told me it would take several buses and a lot of tolerance to reach my destination.

At RAF Ringwell, a guard patrolled the front entrance. He marched back and forth with the intelligence of a metronome. The guard stood six feet and towered over my featherweight frame. He scrutinised my papers with the diligence of a building society manager with a mortgage application.

'Fuck off,' I said impatiently. 'I don't have all day and I want to get some grub.'

'All right, all right, can't be too careful these days with who we are going to let in, ya know.'

The guard stood down and let me pass. I swaggered past him and in a parting gesture thrust my two right fingers upwards. Past the gate, Ringwell expanded into an encampment many times larger than Fuhlsbüttel. Trucks barrelled past and churned up snow and gravel that splashed against my greatcoat. The further I walked into the camp, the louder the racket became. Coming from the parade ground, I heard sergeants barking at teenage boys who were being squad-bashed into submission.

I presented my transfer papers to a lieutenant. He had light-coloured hair and effeminate hands, and looked like he had got his commission before he was given permission to shave. His young face had a disdainful countenance. It appeared as if he found his Manchester billet an unappetising location, a barbarous place compared to Kent or Sussex.

In an Oxbridge accent, he told me: 'You'll find we do things differently here. This is not Germany. I expect discipline and order and no funny business with the natives if you get my meaning.'

'Natives?' I asked. I thought perhaps this camp in Manchester was surrounded by Picts and Saxons from the dark ages.

'You know full well what I mean. I've heard what you enlisted men got up to in Germany with the black market and the girls.'

Inside, I grimaced and grew rigid. 'Terrible business that was, sir; the lower ranks were like the dish that made off with the spoon.'

The newly commissioned officer grumbled. 'Yes, well, none of that here.'

'Sir, will I be permanently stationed here?' I asked.

'Nothing is permanent. There are problems all over the empire; who knows where you shall end up? We've got you for another three years. So I imagine you're going to see quite a bit of the world before your time is done with us.'

That was the last thing I wanted to hear. 'Excuse me, sir, but the reason for my asking is because I'm married and my wife is still in Germany.'

'Married a Hun, eh? Well, that's your problem. The RAF takes care of our own. Wives are a different matter. She can follow you here, but if you are going into a combat zone, she's out of luck.'

The officer turned silent, as if he had forgotten his script from the officer's training course he had taken at Oxford.

'Sir?' I asked.

'Oh, the sergeant outside will see to your kip and your duties.'

I saluted, stamped my feet, and turned smartly out of his office.

'Lucky days for you, Smith,' the sergeant in the foyer told me. 'We've got the best assignment for a man of your brainy character.'

'I'm sure,' I said. 'Go on, let's have it.'

'We've put you in charge of a squad of lads who are as thick as treacle. We've got brave and dangerous work for you and your boys.'

'Come again?'

'There are about 100,000 – nah, maybe ten times more than that; who knows the numbers ...'

'100,000 what?' I asked, puzzled.

'Radio receivers and transmitters, lad, and we need them all smashed to kingdom come.'

'Why?'

'Cos the government bought 'em off the Yanks during the war and the toffs probably spent £20 million on them. So, now it's time to destroy them. Surely you can get it through your noggin that the stuffed shirts don't want them in the hands of Mrs Jones on Kettle Way. It might upset the radio manufacturers or it might lead to mutiny if they got into the hands of the colonies.'

'I was transferred from Germany for this?'

'Sure. From your service records, it says you are a good wireless operator. So you are going to be a brilliant radio basher. Any questions?'

'Just one: how do I get out of this mad house?'

My feeling of gloom didn't get any better when night arrived. I went to my sleeping quarters, which was a banged-up old Nissen hut filled with fresh and unblemished raw recruits. Children, I thought when I got a look at them. They had experienced the war and its aftermath by a coal fire, while their mothers fetched them tea. I must have looked like a pensioner to them.

As much as I wanted to fall asleep, I couldn't. There was just too much alteration to my life in one day. It was like being thrown back to the first days of my induction at the start of the war. I tried dreaming of the curve of Friede's back, the smell of her hair, or the smile from her lips. It didn't work. It made things worse. The images of my wife evaporated like advertisement billboards at the side of a road. Thinking of her just made the longing worse. I closed my eyes again and wanted just blackness to curtain my heart and my head. I rolled over; the boy in the bed beside me snored and farted through the night. To the other side was a habitual sleep-talker. His somnolent conversations appeared to be as dull as his waking intercourse with others. Throughout the twilight hours, I clutched my pillow as if it were the neck of the Air Ministry. I silently repeated as it if were the catechism: I am in the shit now. How am I to get out of this mess?

Morning came abruptly and ugly. An NCO introduced us back to consciousness with the familiar scream of 'Wakey, wakey, sunshine!'

It was both cold and dark and no one had thought to light the stove. I scrambled out for a cigarette. The American fag sparked me to life as the nicotine burrowed into my blood. I decided it was time to collect my duty roster.

After breakfast, I made my way to the parade ground. A sergeant ordered me to assemble the 28 recruits who were listed in my work detail manifest. I was ordered to march them to a work shed located at the far end of the camp.

'It's a mile down the roadway to the smashing and bashing shop,' said a sergeant. 'You'll find enough work there to keep you and yer lads busy till kingdom bloody come. We've got more radios than dogs on this island.'

I assembled my 28 men on the parade ground, while behind us the Union Jack flapped furiously against an angry winter wind.

Before we left, I ordered the men to gather sledgehammers from a storehouse to assist in their Luddite occupation.

I quick-stepped them towards the work shed with a clipboard resting underneath my armpit like a major's riding crop.

The men moved with too much excitement and too much racket from the parade square. 'Shut it!' I screamed. I was irritated by their enthusiasm because it was the kind of eagerness that only an eighteen-year-old can muster at the thought of a day's pay for a day's destruction.

My work detail proceeded with inane determination to the warehouse where the surplus receivers awaited their execution. Upon arrival, I was greeted by another LAC who told me: 'I hope you brought a book because the last man who was in charge of this project went stark raving mad from the bleeding boredom.'

He took me inside and showed me around the building.

The warehouse was divided into two rooms; one was stacked with disused radios, while the other had a series of tables and chairs.

'At the end of the day,' said the LAC, 'a truck will pull up to the back of the building where your men are to load the busted pieces into the wagon.'

He handed me a cigarette and asked, 'Any questions?' I shook my head and thanked him. As he left, the LAC shouted back to me: 'Remember, it doesn't matter how fast or slow you do this job because it's going to be yours, for the rest of your life.'

My men worked in teams and opened up the back of the receivers to remove the radio tubes, which were to be stored in wooden boxes. The castrated transmitters and receivers were then placed onto the concrete floor and a team of men with sledgehammers crushed them beyond recognition.

For the first few days, I walked around the demolition site like a foreman inspecting the labour of skilled journeymen. With a keen look, I observed my men while they smashed thousands of pounds' worth of radio equipment. I congratulated brawny men for their hammer-swinging acumen. 'Put some passion behind it, man,' I told one new recruit as he lazily swung his hammer.

Each day walked into the next day with the same banging routine. For eight hours a day, I sat behind a desk. I took my scheduled tea break and returned diligently to supervise the wrecking of equipment that was considered too expensive to keep but too cheap to sell. I wondered how much we borrowed during the war from the Americans to buy these receivers, only to destroy them in peacetime. Whatever the price, I knew the debt was still outstanding. We were still paying for lend-lease. We were still paying for Churchill's exhortation to defend our island, 'whatever the cost may be.' The arrears were enormous and our nation still suffered from rationing. We were rich in war and poor in peace.

Day in, day out, I marched the men to our workplace and ordered them to do their duty. I observed them hammer, bang, and crush radio receivers to dust. My ears rang and I drowned in the noise created by our obligation to the state. With every hour that I endured this destruction, I reasoned, I had gained another 60 minutes to scheme and find a solution to end my suffering, my sodding contract to the RAF.

Each day, I wrote letters to Friede in Germany. I tried to lower her expectations of what life was to be like in Britain. I wrote that it was very different from Hamburg, but I promised that our life in Yorkshire was still going to be pleasant. It would still be filled with excitement. Each night, I went to bed knowing that I was lying to her and fooling myself if I believed life would be as good as in Germany. Each morning, I woke wondering how peace had become a battle for me and my nation. This peace, this hard-fought peace, was as dark and as terrible as the days in the Great Depression. I was like a fish on a hook, wriggling and squirming trying to get the metal barb out of my throat and instead it plunged deeper into my flesh.

No matter how hard I fought to escape my present, no matter how much I planned for my future, the hammers came down and the dust flew up from the splintered and crushed corpses of the radio receivers. My ears stung from the pounding and my spirit almost broke from the pointlessness of my task. At break time, I sipped weak tea in a chipped mug and dreamed of that beautiful spring at the end of the war in 1945. I dreamed of the spring to come, when I could buy my way out of the RAF and be reunited with Friede.

The only problem was, even in my dreams I was afraid and I was alone. There was no one to confess my terror and dread that my luck had run out. I recoiled in despair, knowing that I was plunging back into my old life in the festering mill town of my youth. Except this time, I was returning with a foreign bride who was not prepared for Yorkshire in all its post-war gloom. I asked myself: How was it possible that after surviving the war and seven years' service in the RAF, I was starting out where I began, except this time I had something to lose? I was petrified of what was to become of me after I got out of Ringwell. All I wanted was a future that was better than my past and the honest chance to find work, to feed myself and my family.

CHAPTER 28

Life begins

With a steady frozen pace, winter crept over the land and over my heart during the last few weeks of 1947. In early December the snow fell hard and heavy and left me morose and missing my former life with Friede in Hamburg.

For Christmas break, I'd been offered leave to return to my Mam's house in Halifax but declined both the RAF's and my mother's invitation. In a letter my sister warned me that our mother was a tempest of vitriol for all who crossed her path, because her boyfriend Bill's roving eye had caught the fancy of a middle-aged barmaid down at their local.

That news, along with my own depressed state, convinced me it was best for both my wallet and my soul to remain behind the barbed wire fence of Ringway RAF base.

So for me and my crew, we marked time with a steady beat of hammer blows, pulverising RAF equipment until December relented and made way for January 1948.

Considering that it was eighteen months since Britain's victory over fascism, my despondency wasn't unique. There were many people like me trying to salvage their lives from the ruins of that miserable war. Britain in the late 1940s was a tough go for many, and personal happiness seemed as tightly rationed as sweets. It was a period of extreme austerity because the new Labour government had to settle our country's war debts and was also beginning to build a social safety network to protect everyone.

All of my boyhood friends also felt put off by this post-war world, and one even wrote to me to say that he felt like a bicycle tyre with a slow leak.

The euphoria of surviving the war intact had dissipated and now I, along with the rest of my generation, knew that to make Britain work, regardless of our station in life, we had to help rebuild the country to suit the needs of our generation. The working class had voted overwhelmingly for a Labour government in 1945, and that administration would give us the keys to the kingdom – but only if we stood up and accepted our responsibility to assist in its creation.

The only problem with Labour's pledge for me and so many others who had been short-changed by poverty, the Great Depression and the Second World War, was that we believed the speed of change was too slow.

Still, regardless of our youthful enthusiasm for Britain to transform into a more egalitarian society, and our impa-tience at the petty pace of change, we knew we'd have to pitch in to make it happen, or else the country's elite would nip this peaceful social revolution in the bud.

So, after a steady media diet of essays from the *Guardian* and *New Statesman* and newsreels that showed my gener-ation literally constructing the welfare state by rebuilding Britain's Blitz-shattered cities, I was convinced that my place was back on Civvy Street.

So one day while I marched my men to the bashing shed, I resolved to buy out my three-year contract with the RAF and be reunited with Friede as soon as possible.

I reasoned that there was more chance of building a stable life for me and her if I wore a worker's smock rather than a blue serge uniform. Besides, I wanted to put down roots and I knew that this peacetime Air Force whose budget had been slashed to help pay for things that mattered – like better schools and hospitals for the soon-to-be opened NHS – wasn't going to accommodate my desire for both comfort and purpose.

At first, my RAF superiors weren't supportive of my desire to buy out my contract with them.

After I announced my intentions to a sergeant, I was berated: 'You like to stir the shit, don't you, Smith? You don't seem to know which side your toast is buttered. First you marry a bloody Hun, and now you want to leave the RAF before your peacetime contract has run its course. I should call you "cut-and-run Harry". That attitude won't do you any favours in the civilian world either.'

But through perseverance, and keeping my cool, I wore down my superiors' reluctance to sign the papers allowing me to end my contract with the RAF and be reunited with Friede. In the end they accepted that I did my bit when my country needed me because I had enlisted in the RAF in 1941 at the age of eighteen.

At the beginning of March the RAF said fair enough and agreed to my demobilisation from the forces. So a little after my 25th birthday, Friede flew from Hamburg to Gatwick and we began the earnest work of trying to make a life for ourselves in a Britain that was changing for the better.

At first, the move to Britain was a difficult transition for Friede. She was cosmopolitan but Halifax, where we settled after I left the RAF, was provincial, stuffy and riddled with class divisions and ancient prejudice against outsiders and new ideas. Friede was not used to the rough-and-tumble world that Britain's working class took for granted and she was shocked at the deprivations ordinary people endured in our country. Still, it didn't take her long to develop a great and abiding love for England and Yorkshire, which was returned by the many people who befriended Friede during our early married years.

In many ways Friede found solace in the circle of friends that had been with me since my boyhood. Many of them had, like me, married women from different parts of the world and this made our fraternity even stronger.

Early on, Friede and I met and became fast friends with a Polish refugee who had fought at Dunkirk and on the beaches of D-Day. He was married to a Belgian woman who became like a sister to Friede. The four of us spent endless weekends rambling across Ilkley Moor, cracking jokes, reciting poems and enjoying the moments that matter when one is young.

Like all young people, newly married, we didn't always understand each other's needs and wants but our love was strong enough to weather the storms of youth and allow us to sail into old age together.

ALSO AVAILABLE

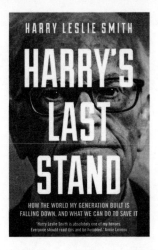

HARRY'S LAST STAND

HOW THE WORLD MY GENERATION BUILT IS FALLING DOWN, AND WHAT WE CAN DO TO SAVE IT

HARRY LESLIE SMITH

'As one of the last remaining survivors of the Great Depression and the Second World War, I will not go gently into that good night. I want to tell you what the world looks like through my eyes, so that you can help change it.' *Harry Leslie Smith*

'Harry Leslie Smith is absolutely one of my heroes. Everyone should read this and be humbled.' *Annie Lennox*

'A kind of epic poem, one that moves from passionate denunciation to intense autobiographical reflection … should be required reading for every MP. The fury and sense of powerlessness that so many people feel at government policy beam out of every page.' *Melissa Benn, Guardian*

'I read *Harry's Last Stand* in a single sitting. Labour should read to get fire in bellies. Tories should read in shame.' *Alastair Campbell*

ISBN 978–184831–736–9
UK £8.99